The Lost Woman: Silenced No More

*A Memoir of Surviving Childhood Sexual Abuse
and Breaking the Silence of Shame*

Erica Young

PEN TO PAPER
PUBLISHING

ISBN (Paperback): 979-8-9953738-2-7
ISBN (Hardcover): 979-8-9953738-4-1
ISBN (eBook): 979-8-9953738-3-4

First Edition

Published by Pen to Paper Publishing
Texas, United States

For permissions, speaking engagements, or media inquiries, contact:
www.ericatrinette.com

Cover design by: Pen to Paper Publishing
Interior formatting by: Pen to Paper Publishing

Printed in the United States of America

Content Advisory

This memoir discusses experiences of childhood sexual abuse, trauma, faith struggles, and the long journey of healing.

While the events described in this book are real, the story is told with care and without graphic detail. My intention is not to shock or retraumatize readers, but to share the truth of my experience in a way that honors both the seriousness of abuse and the hope that healing is possible.

For some readers—especially survivors of abuse—certain topics may be emotionally difficult. Please read at your own pace and take breaks if needed. If at any time the content feels overwhelming, it is okay to step away and return when you feel ready.

If you are currently navigating the effects of trauma, you may find it helpful to read alongside a trusted friend, counselor, or support system. There is also a companion journal available, Silenced No More: A Personal Healing Journey, that may help you process your own emotions as you move through this memoir.

If you or someone you know is experiencing abuse or needs support, please consider reaching out to a trusted professional or a local support organization. There are resources provided in the back of this book.

My hope is that this story reminds survivors that they are not alone, that their voices matter, and that healing—though often slow and difficult—is possible.

Author's Note

The story you are about to read is deeply personal. It is a memoir of survival, faith, healing, and the long journey toward freedom after childhood sexual abuse.

While the events shared in these pages are true, some names and identifying details have been changed to protect the privacy of individuals and families. My intention in writing this book is not to shame or expose anyone, but to tell my story honestly and to offer hope to others who may be walking a similar path.

For many years, this story lived in silence.

Silence born out of fear.
Silence born out of confusion.
Silence born out of shame that was never mine to carry.

Over time, through faith, counseling, and the support of safe people, I began to understand that silence often protects the wrong things. It protects the harm. It protects the secrecy. And it keeps survivors from discovering the freedom that comes with healing.

Writing this memoir required careful reflection. Some moments were painful to revisit, while others reminded me of the incredible ways God has brought healing and restoration into my life. I have done my best to tell this story with dignity and grace—honoring both the truth of what happened and the healing that has taken place since.

This book does not contain graphic descriptions of abuse. My goal is not to retraumatize readers but to share my journey in a way that acknowledges the reality of trauma while also pointing toward the possibility of healing.

If you are a survivor of abuse, my hope is that you find encouragement within these pages. Healing is not a straight path, and it does not happen overnight. But it is possible.

You are not alone.

If you are reading this as a parent, friend, counselor, or advocate, I hope this story provides insight into the complex journey many survivors walk and the importance of compassion, patience, and safe support.

Above all, this book is a testimony of redemption. It is evidence that God can bring beauty from ashes and that what was meant for harm does not have to define the rest of a life.

For many years, I believed my story would end in silence.

Today, I know that silence does not get the final word.

Table of Contents

Epilogue — Forgiveness Does Not Always Equal Reconciliation

Acknowledgment

Seventeen

My father once told me that if I wanted to leave when I turned seventeen, I could.

It wasn't a long conversation. It was more of a statement, something said in passing. But when you grow up in a house where most of the decisions about your life are not really yours to make, even a sentence like that can feel like hope.

I held on to those words for years.

Seventeen became more than just another birthday. In my mind, it became the day everything would change. The day I would finally have the freedom to make decisions for myself. The day I could step away from a life that often felt like it belonged more to someone else than it did to me.

Silenced No More

I counted the years.

Then the months.

Eventually, the days.

I imagined what it might feel like to breathe without constantly wondering if I was about to do something wrong. I imagined what it would be like to make a decision without asking permission first. I imagined what life might look like if I didn't feel like someone else was always watching, always controlling, always deciding what was best for me.

For a long time, I believed him.

When you grow up under control, you learn to hold on to even the smallest pieces of hope. Sometimes hope looks like a promise. Sometimes it looks like a date on the calendar.

For me, hope looked like seventeen.

But freedom, as I would learn, was never really the plan.

I remember the day everything shifted.

I was standing in the parking lot of a post office when the promise I had held on to for so long started to unravel right in front of me. The man who had controlled so much of my life began calling me names.

I remember the humiliation more than the words themselves.

People were walking in and out of the building behind us, going about their normal day, while my world felt like it was shrinking right there in that parking lot.

In that moment, something became painfully clear.

The freedom I thought I had been promised was never really mine to claim.

It had only been another way to keep control.

I left that day feeling smaller than I had in a long time, unsure of what my future actually looked like and uncertain about how much power I really had over my own life.

Four years passed.

Four years of trying to figure out what freedom actually meant for me.

Then one day, I found myself staring down at a pregnancy test.

Two pink lines.

Everything around me in that moment felt both quiet and loud at the same time.

For most of my life, my choices had been shaped by someone else's control, someone else's expectations, and someone else's actions. But as I stood there holding that test in my hands, something inside me shifted.

For the first time, the decision in front of me was not just about my own survival.

It was about protecting someone else.

And deep down, I knew something I had not been able to say out loud before.

Silenced No More

If I didn't find an escape now, I might never be able to leave at all.

What I did not fully understand at the time was how long silence had already been shaping my life.

That silence had begun years earlier.

Long before I ever turned seventeen.

Part 1

The First Silence

CHAPTER 1

The First Silence

I remember being around five years old, playing with my father. I think my little brother, Jerome, and my big sister, Kita, were there, too. I was having fun, laughing, and playing as children do. Then I remember my father saying something about my underarms smelling bad.

My feelings were hurt, and I started to cry.

My father's reasoning was that it was better for me to hear something like that from him than from a stranger. In his mind, he was trying to protect me. And I believed him, but protection would take on a different meaning over the years.

Some of my earliest memories feel confusing when I look back on them now. I would love to say that I remember many good things before innocence was taken from me, but the truth is that parts of my story were already complicated long before I understood what any of it meant.

My life story had already been affected by circumstances beyond my control the day I was born.

I was the product of a man and his mistress. I didn't know it at the time. Some of my earliest memories are being in my childhood home, and both my parents being present.

Of course, I had no say in the matter, but it would matter in my story as time went by.

My father attended a local church where he was a deacon. I wouldn't go to his church until years later. When I was younger, my mom often took my siblings and me to her church. We attended a Pentecostal Church, and it felt like we were always there.

Sometimes it was fun. Even at a young age, I enjoyed parts of it—the music, the energy, and the sense that something important was happening around us.

But even then, I could sense that I didn't quite fit in. Although I went to church with other children, I didn't live nearby, as most of them did. They saw each other during the week and built friendships outside of church.

Because of that, I never felt as close to them as they seemed to be with each other. Even as a preteen, I noticed those differences.

It often felt like the only place I truly belonged was with my siblings at home.

My home consisted of my mom, my older brother, my older sister, my younger brother, and me.

Even though we fought sometimes, we understood each other. And my older brother, Dedrick, was my hero.

As I got older, things between my parents became more complicated. What had once seemed normal to me began to feel uncertain, even though I didn't fully understand why at the time.

Eventually, unbeknownst to me, my father and his then-wife divorced. He and my mom continued to see each other for a while, but one night something happened that shredded whatever was left of their relationship.

"Call the police!"

I was about nine years old when I woke up to those words. To this day, I don't know why none of my siblings heard it, but I did.

Still half asleep, I walked toward my mother's voice and grabbed the phone. But when I realized who I would be calling the police on, I froze.

It was my father.

I don't know what had happened before I walked in, rubbing my sleepy eyes, but my father seemed scared. He walked toward me and tried to hold me and convince me to put the phone down.

In that moment, confusion rushed in.

Honor thy father and thy mother… but what if honoring one means dishonoring the other?

That felt like an impossible decision for a nine-year-old to make.

In the end, I didn't call the police, and my father left.

It wasn't long before we realized that Mom and Dad were no longer together. He stopped coming over to stay the night. Seeing him now meant going to spend weekends with him and his new live-in girlfriend.

That became the new normal.

His girlfriend seemed nice. She worked at a place that made good food, and she would sometimes pick me up from school if I said I wasn't feeling well.

For a while, she became a regular part of our lives.

Time went by, and like many other weekends, my little brother and I went to stay with our father.

My father spent time with me and made me feel loved—or at least what I believed at the time was love.

I would later learn that something else had been happening.

He had been grooming me to become what he would later call his "child bride." Because I was so attached to him and had no other example of how a father behaves, nothing he said initially seemed wrong to me.

After all, he was a deacon in the church. He was respected by many people in the community, and he often talked about hearing from God. He would tell me about things God had supposedly shared with him.

Everything about his life seemed to reinforce the idea that he was a man of authority and integrity.

Even the authorities appeared to think highly of him—or at least that's how it seemed. They didn't even bring him in for questioning when the abuse charges were first mentioned.

Yes, I did say something.

But that part of the story will come later.

Before anything sexual ever happened, my father would sometimes have pornography playing on the television. At the time, I didn't understand what I was seeing.

Now, as an adult, I believe it was an intentional part of his grooming process.

One particular morning stands out in my memory.

After my father took his live-in girlfriend to work, he brought me into his bedroom. He began touching my body and guiding me toward his bed. After laying me down, he pressed his body on top of mine and began moving inappropriately in a grinding motion—almost like trying to have sex while our clothes were still on.

Shortly after it started, my body began to feel tingly. It was a strange feeling, one I couldn't control.

Years later, I would learn that my body had experienced an orgasm.

My father understood what had happened.

Silenced No More

I did not.

I remember feeling confused more than anything else. Not just about what had happened, but about why it had happened. I didn't know if I had done something wrong or if I was supposed to understand it in a way I simply couldn't yet.

After a moment, he lifted himself off of me. I quietly walked back to the room where I had been sleeping before all of this happened. My brother was still asleep on the bed.

Confused about what had happened, but almost certain that something about it was not okay, I climbed into bed beside him and curled up behind him.

I stayed there quietly, almost as if being close to him could somehow make me feel safe again. It was almost as if I needed him to protect me—even though he didn't know it.

I didn't wake him up. I didn't know what to say, so I said nothing. Instead, I just lay there, trying to make sense of something I didn't understand, while trying to act as if everything was still normal.

Years later, my little brother would tell me he remembered that day and how scared I seemed, curled up behind him. He just didn't know why.

Like normal, my father took us back to our mom's house when the weekend ended.

But I didn't go home empty-handed.

Along with my bag of clothes and belongings, I carried something else with me—confusion and uncertainty.

Home looked the same. My siblings were the same, and so was my mom.

But, I wasn't.

Even though I couldn't explain what had changed, I knew something inside me had shifted in a way I couldn't undo.

I didn't have the words for it then, only a quiet instinct that whatever had taken place was not something a child should experience.

From that point on, whenever my father came to pick us up for the weekend, only my little brother would go.

By choice, I stayed behind. I didn't fully understand why I no longer wanted to go, but something in me knew I didn't feel safe anymore. It wasn't something I knew how to explain out loud. I tried to act like everything was normal, but in reality, everything had changed.

Eventually, my mom asked me if everything was okay.

I didn't know if I could tell her or if I should. Still unsure of what to say, I simply told her that I wanted to stay home with her. That was an easier answer than trying to explain something I didn't yet have the words or comprehension for.

Although she didn't seem completely convinced, she accepted that answer—at least for a while.

Silenced No More

Until the truth came out.

CHAPTER 2

When the World Became Unsafe

Time went on, and even though I knew something about that morning was not right, life didn't stop. I still had to go to school, be around my sister and brothers, and dodge the questions my mom kept asking.

Fear and shame were already making their presence known, even though I didn't yet know their names.

I also had to see my father whenever he came to pick up my little brother. It always felt strange, but I didn't have the words to explain why. Looking back now, I realize my body already knew something was wrong, even though my mind was still trying to understand it.

Life kept moving, and I tried not to think about what had happened. In many ways, I had almost pushed it out of my mind.

Until the day my sister and I decided to play a game we called "secrets."

While playing "secrets" with my big sister, we took turns sharing things and laughing. At first, the game was light and funny. But then everything changed.

I realized I had a secret to tell, one that I knew my sister wouldn't guess. I didn't fully understand what I was about to reveal, but there would be no turning back.

I didn't want to say it out loud, wasn't sure that I really wanted to share it, so I wrote it down on a piece of paper and handed it to my sister. I remember smiling, waiting for her to laugh with me so we could continue the game.

And for a moment, time seemed to stand still. Looking visibly bothered and saying very few initial words, I could tell my sister didn't like my secret.

I didn't understand the magnitude of what had taken place months prior on that early morning at my father's house.

But my sister did. She was three years older, and her level of understanding was more mature than mine.

After reading what I wrote, she looked at me and asked if it was true. When I said yes, she immediately told me that what had happened was not okay. I could see it not only in her words, but also in her reaction. Still unsure of what it all meant, the situation felt more confusing.

She contacted our older brother, Dedrick, and told him everything. Because my mom was a single mother, my brother often stepped into the role of authority when she was at work or away from home.

When he heard what had happened, he was furious.

I didn't understand everything that was being said, and I still hadn't realized how wrong what had been done to me really was. But I knew something was very wrong based on my brother's reaction. He had contacted some other family members and friends, and they were ready to go find my father and confront him.

Before that could happen, my mom was told what had taken place. She called the police, and within a short time, they were standing on our front porch, ready to take my statement.

I was nervous and confused, but I told them what my father had done. I didn't know what would happen afterwards. I don't know that I had any expectations.

Shouldn't that have been the end of it?

It wasn't.

I don't remember the police coming back or asking for additional information. There were no updates and no arrests. That silence and lack of follow through said more than words ever could.

The words that I do remember came in the form of the talk around town.

Silenced No More

The town was small, and everyone seemed to know everyone else's business—including mine.

One of the first times I was questioned about what had happened was during choir practice in Bethlehem, Mississippi. I remember the other children gathering around me, curious about the story they had heard.

They wanted details.

I remember adding things to the story when they asked questions. Looking back, I sometimes wonder why I did that. Was the truth not enough? Was I simply responding to what I thought they wanted to hear? Or was I reacting to things they had already heard adults saying around them?

Maybe it was a combination of all of those things.

Either way, it made everything worse.

They weren't asking because they cared. They were curious children who had heard something shocking and wanted to know more. Instead of finding support, I found myself becoming the subject of whispers, teasing, and bullying. I had become someone to talk about when I should have been someone people were trying to care for.

I already felt I was not considered the pretty one. I didn't wear the latest fashions. Now, in their minds, I was someone to talk about, someone to avoid, someone to make fun of.

And this was still elementary school.

Junior high and high school were still years away.

The bullying had already begun in elementary school, but after people learned what had happened, it intensified. In a small town, news traveled quickly. I knew parents had talked about it in front of their children because kids my age seemed to know things they shouldn't have known.

At school, during choir practice, and even around the neighborhood, other kids asked questions, made cruel comments, or tried to take advantage of my vulnerability.

There were days when I ran home from school just to avoid being confronted or bullied by other kids in the neighborhood.

I tried to act cool and make decisions I thought would help me fit in. Sometimes I allowed attention from boys that crossed boundaries I didn't yet understand how to protect.

After a while, it seemed easier to go along with people's expectations than to constantly defend myself against rumors and assumptions about who I was.

In many ways, I think I just wanted the focus to shift away from what my father had done.

But in a small town, stories linger.

After a while, and I don't know exactly how it came to be, but I was sent back with my father for a day visit.

It was flea market weekend.

The flea market was a place we had gone many times before. Back then, it had always felt like a normal outing. But this time everything felt different.

Silenced No More

Everything felt awkward.

At one point, I wandered off by myself to look around the flea market. After a while, I became thirsty, so I went to find my father to ask for the one or two dollars it would cost to buy a lemonade.

His money came with a condition.

He wanted to know why I had told on him for what he did.

"Nobody would have known if you had never said anything," he said.

I didn't have an answer.

We stood there for a moment that felt much longer than it probably was. After that awkward silence, he handed me the money for the drink, and I walked away.

But the question stayed with me longer than the moment itself.

It made me question myself.

Had I misunderstood everything that happened?

Confusion settled in deeper than before.

Had my sister blown the situation out of proportion?

I mean…he hadn't "hurt" me.

The police hadn't arrested him.

Had he actually done something wrong, or was I the one who was confused?

After all, he was my father.

And fathers were supposed to love their children.

I don't think many words were spoken on the way home that day.

For a while, things seemed normal again. My little brother and I resumed going to my father's house on weekends.

Then, gradually, he began touching me again.

It didn't happen all at once. It was subtle at first, almost like he was testing to see if I would say anything this time.

Touches turned into kisses.

And kisses eventually turned into full-blown molestation.

By then, he had convinced me that what he was doing was "God's will," and that God was pleased with what was happening.

Over time, he also convinced me that I couldn't tell anyone, because other people wouldn't understand what God had ordained.

And I believed him.

I didn't know I had the right not to.

My father had already begun shaping how I understood truth, authority, and even God.

Truth slowly became lies, and lies slowly became truth. If my father said something was true, no one else could convince me otherwise.

Besides, he told me he was protecting me.

So, I became very good at keeping our secret and living a double life.

By the time I was twelve years old, I was a deeply confused young girl whose only understanding of sex had been shaped by what my father called "God's will."

I didn't know I wasn't supposed to just go along with the advances of others.

And I didn't yet understand that I had the right to say no.

I had already been labeled as strange or different by kids at school. Now, there were new labels added to the list. I was called ugly, weird, nasty, and unwanted.

Over time, those words began to translate into something deeper inside of me.

Unwanted.
Unloved.
Unworthy.

I learned to live with those labels, even though they were never truly mine to carry.

Elementary school eventually ended, but junior high brought new challenges—more confusion, more pressure, and new rumors about who I was.

Around the beginning of seventh grade, I spent time at my brother's girlfriend's house. This was one of my siblings on my father's side that I had gotten to know of in recent years. For a few weeks, I had been talking on the phone with her stepbrother, and I thought I liked him.

One evening, we were there together, and poor choices were made. I found myself in a situation where I agreed to something I did not fully understand or think through. At the time, I did not see it as a serious decision. In my mind, it was simply something that had happened.

But the story spread quickly.

In a small town, it didn't take long for people to hear about it and form their opinions. Suddenly, I was being called another name—one I had heard before but never imagined would be attached to me.

People began labeling me based on that single moment, stacked on top of the rumors about my father.

When I went to school, I could hear people whispering and talking about me. Boys no longer saw me as someone worth respecting, and I remember feeling deeply confused by it all.

What had I done that was so terrible?

I still remember coming home from school one afternoon. My older brother, Dedrick, and some of his friends were in the backyard playing basketball. When he saw me, he was furious. He didn't want me anywhere near them.

Again, I was confused.

But in a small town, word travels quickly, and apparently, everyone already knew what had happened.

Looking back, I can see how that moment kept me stuck in perfection mode for years afterward. I spent a long time trying to prove that one incident did not define me and that I was still worthy of love and acceptance.

But at the time, it felt like another mark had been placed on my life.

As if the labels I already carried weren't enough, this experience seemed to confirm what others already believed about me.

I didn't yet understand why my choices were wrong or how deeply my understanding of boundaries had already been distorted.

In many ways, I was only repeating what had been taught to me without words—that saying yes was expected, and that my body was not truly my own.

I can see how quickly the world around me changed after the truth came out. What had once been simple childhood experiences were suddenly overshadowed by rumors, questions, and labels I did not yet understand.

The world had become a place where innocence could disappear quickly, and silence often felt safer than speaking the truth.

Because I was learning the lesson life was teaching me: even in telling the truth, safety wasn't guaranteed.

CHAPTER 3

Shame's Voice

Shortly after the incident in seventh grade, things changed again.

When I was thirteen, my father told me that we were entering into what he called a marriage covenant. He had me place my hand on the Bible and repeat words that he said formed a covenant between him, God, and me.

I didn't understand what I was agreeing to at that moment. I just knew it felt serious. The way he spoke about it made it feel sacred and special, like something I wasn't supposed to question or take lightly.

To make it feel real, he even went to the local Walmart and bought me a gold ring. I wore it on my ring finger for years.

At the time, it didn't feel strange in the way it should have. It felt normal because he had made it normal. There are pictures from middle school and high school where that ring can clearly be seen.

But, that's what manipulation does. It reshapes what should feel wrong into something that feels expected.

According to him, the condition of this "marriage" was that I would be free when I turned seventeen—if I chose to be.

The only explanation he gave was a story from the Bible about Lot and his daughters. He twisted a Biblical story to his advantage and claimed it provided justification. He claimed God had no problem with what he was doing. At thirteen years old, I did not know how to question what he told me. He had groomed me since I was a small child, had been abusing me for years, and was known in the community as a respected church deacon. People believed he heard from God. At thirteen years old, why wouldn't I believe him, too?

I did not know how to question his interpretation of the Bible. I didn't have another voice strong enough to challenge his. And when one voice is all you hear, it starts to sound like truth.

There I was—thirteen years old and convinced that I was bound to my father by a covenant that God somehow approved.

In some ways, another role was about to be added to my life— one I never expected at thirteen.

In April of 2000, I became an aunt, by way of one of my big brothers on my father's side. I was there from the very beginning.

I saw him often, and at one point, my nephew and his parents even lived with my father. That meant I was able to spend even more time with him.

Even though I was still a teenager myself, I quickly became very connected to my nephew. As time went on, I found myself caring for him more and more. His parents would go places and leave him with my father and me. Sometimes my father would leave as well, and my nephew and I would end up back at my mother's house together. He was not related to my mom, but she would let me watch him at her house sometimes.

Life continued to happen. My brother, who was my nephew's father, was eventually sent to prison, and my nephew's mother had her own struggles. What began as occasional babysitting slowly started to feel more like raising a child of my own—even though I had never given birth.

I remember countless nights rocking him to sleep, changing diapers, feeding him, bathing him, and taking him almost everywhere with me. Anyone who has cared for a baby knows about those long nights when you want to sleep but can't. And I was doing this as a thirteen-year-old.

Sometimes he even came with me to basketball games. As a teenager, walking into a gymnasium with an infant in a car seat was not exactly the coolest thing, but life kept moving forward, and I did what needed to be done.

As he got older, he stayed close to me. There were mornings when I would drive twenty minutes to take him to his bus stop before heading to school myself. And yes, I was only thirteen and driving. In the small Mississippi town where I grew up, that wasn't unusual. Driving young was simply part of life there.

In the afternoons, I would leave school in time to pick him up again. On days when I had track practice, he would come back to the gym with me and sit on the sidelines while I practiced. Eventually, my coach and teammates expected to see him there. Some of them would even play with him while I trained and kept him entertained.

For years, I found myself stepping into the role of caregiver again and again—a child helping raise another child.

One day, he asked if he could call me "mom." I knew he had a mother, but I remember feeling something warm inside when he asked. I was still too young to fully understand what it meant to be someone's mother, but being there for him felt natural and gave me purpose. After feeling unworthy and lacking confidence, it felt good knowing at least one person felt I was needed and lovable.

In a life where so much felt confusing and out of my control, caring for him gave me something that felt steady.

For a long time, having him with me became normal, and in many ways, I wouldn't have had it any other way.

Looking back now, I think it was easier focusing on him than thinking about what was happening to me.

While life on the outside appeared normal, the abuse continued and, in many ways, intensified.

My father's demands for my body intensified, and he wasn't always asking. There were nights when I would babysit my nephew and niece. Sometimes I tried to keep the children awake longer than necessary because I knew that as long as they were awake, my father would stay away. But eventually the house would grow quiet, and the tension would build.

One night stands out clearly in my memory. It was already dark outside, and my father kept coming in and out of the room to check if the children were asleep yet. I knew what he was waiting for.

I tried to wait it out and hope that somehow the night would pass without anything happening.

Eventually, he walked in with anger in his eyes. He picked up the small television in the room and lifted it as if he were about to throw it. In that moment, I was terrified. I do not remember what I said or did—maybe nothing at all—but after a moment, he set the television back down and walked out of the room.

That was only one of many nights where fear hung in the air.

Fear didn't always come with noise. Many times, it came with silence.

Over time, I learned what to say and what not to say. I learned how to read his moods. I learned how to avoid making things worse. In ways I didn't fully understand at the time, I was learning how to survive.

As the years passed, other people began noticing that I was either at my mother's house or with my father. When I wasn't with him, he often drove past my mother's house as if checking to make sure I was there.

Unfortunately, vulnerability attracts predators.

Two acquaintances of my older brother, Dedrick, began coming around and taking advantage of my situation. While my mom was at work, on different days, one of them would stop by to see my brother, but if he wasn't there, they would linger.

At the time, I did not fully understand what was happening. To me, it simply became another secret to carry. I didn't know how to recognize danger. My understanding of boundaries had already been broken, and I didn't yet know how to put them back in place. I hadn't yet realized the boundaries were broken.

Many years later, I realized what had been happening was a crime. Grown men had seen me, a vulnerable and confused girl, heard whispers about what was happening in my life, and instead of protecting me, they chose to exploit me as well.

By that point, I had already learned to be a people pleaser. I had learned to say yes in situations where I did not feel safe saying no. I did not know how to stop what was happening, and part of me believed that if people were paying attention to me, it meant they cared about me.

Looking back now, I can see how wrong that thinking was.

They were not showing kindness or concern. They were taking advantage of a child who had already been deeply harmed.

My father became aware that these men were coming around. He wanted the situation to stop, but confronting them would have meant exposing himself. Explaining why their actions were wrong would have forced him to admit that what he had been doing to me for years was wrong, too.

I do not remember exactly how long that situation lasted, but I do remember the moment everything changed.

July 1, 2001, is a date I will never forget. It was the last day I would ever see my brother Dedrick alive.

We were never given the full details of what happened. What we were told was that he had drowned while trying to save someone else. Just like that, he was gone, and there was nothing anyone in our family could do to bring him back.

I was devastated.

Someone stable in my life had been taken away.

The house felt different after he was gone. The person who had once stood between me and the world in small but meaningful ways was no longer there. I did not yet realize how much his presence had protected me until I had to live without it.

As a fourteen-year-old who was secretly enduring abuse almost every day of my life, my brother had been my closest earthly protector. Whether he knew everything that was happening or not, he was someone who tried to look out for me when others did not.

His death changed something inside of me.

Until then, death had felt like something distant—something that happened to older people. Losing him made me realize that life could end suddenly, even for someone young and strong.

After the funeral, my father used my grief as another opportunity to control the narrative of my life. He told me that the involvement with those other men was sinful and that if I died while continuing those actions, I would go to hell. According to him, the only relationship that God had "blessed" was the one between him and me.

As disturbing as it may sound now, I believed him.

I was a grieving fourteen-year-old who had been manipulated for years. His words felt authoritative and final.

When those men came around again, I began making excuses. I avoided being available. I found reasons not to be alone with them. And eventually, they stopped.

My father had succeeded in explaining them away—without ever admitting the truth about himself. They also could no longer use the excuse that they were coming to see my brother.

From that point on, I tried to live as carefully as possible. Decisions, words, and interactions were being filtered through the question: *Will this make things worse?*

I wanted to do what was right. I wanted to avoid making anyone angry. I wanted to stay on what I thought was the straight and narrow path.

But I was trying to follow rules built on lies.

Life continued moving forward. On the outside, I appeared to be a model daughter, a good student, and a dedicated athlete. I went to school, excelled academically, did my chores at my mom's house, and tried to get along with most people.

But beneath the surface, shame had already begun shaping the way I saw myself and the world around me. Most days were about existing in the safest way possible.

Looking back now, I can see how those years quietly shaped the way I understood love, faith, and worth. I believed obedience meant silence, that survival meant pleasing others, and that my value depended on how well I kept the peace.

Shame had begun writing a story about who I was long before I had the courage to question whether that story was even true.

It told me who I was and what I was worth, and for a long time I believed it.

Part 2

When Silence Took Root

CHAPTER 4

The Weight of Secrets

On the outside, my life began to look impressive. I had once again become a model daughter, a committed student, and a dedicated athlete. But beneath the surface, my reality was far more complicated than anyone could see.

Sometimes I wonder if people noticed the changes in me. In some ways, I know they did.

Before the abuse began, I had been a model student. I earned academic awards, had strong relationships with my teachers, and was mostly a fun, shy kid trying to find my place.

After the abuse started, things shifted. In fifth grade, I began acting out in ways that confused the adults around me. I was getting suspended, struggling to get along with some teachers, and often felt like I didn't belong with students my own age.

On one occasion, when I had been suspended, my mother took me to my grandfather's house—her father. He was not pleased about the suspension. I remember him making a comment that a good whipping would probably help me "act right."

I remember hearing that and feeling like something in me shut down even more. I didn't know how to explain that a whipping wouldn't help me.

I couldn't tell him that I disagreed. That would have been seen as disrespectful. Instead, I took on more opinions of others about who I was and what was wrong with me.

Looking back now, I understand why he might have thought that. My behavior had changed dramatically.

What he didn't know was why.

At the time, I didn't have the words to explain that sudden behavior changes in children often come from trauma. I simply carried the confusion and pain quietly.

I didn't speak up as much. I paid more attention to what people thought, and I tried not to stand out in ways that would bring more negative attention my way.

Rumors, though not as in my face as before, still traveled quickly through our small town, and my reputation seemed to grow larger than my actual life. Looking back now, I sometimes wonder about the adults who must have heard those rumors. If people suspected something was wrong, why didn't anyone pick up the phone and call for help?

Maybe they didn't want to believe something like that was actually going on in our town.

By the time I reached junior high, I decided to try out for the cross-country team. Not because I loved running, but because one of the popular girls in my grade planned to try out. I thought maybe it would help me fit in with the "cool" crowd.

But something unexpected happened.

The popular girl eventually stopped coming, and I kept showing up.

Running gave me something to focus on. It gave me a place to put my energy and process my frustration. Before long, I also joined the track team—and it turned out I had real potential. For a few hours a day, I didn't have to think about home life. I could just focus on running.

I was still getting into trouble from time to time, though.

I remember one meeting with administrators and coaching staff where they gave me an ultimatum.

"Erica, you're talented," one of them told me. "But if your behavior doesn't change, you're going to miss out on opportunities. You have a choice to make."

Those words stayed with me.

That was one of the first times someone connected my behavior to my potential.

They didn't know what I was dealing with, but they saw something in me worth protecting, even if they didn't realize that's what they were doing.

Part of my motivation to change was simple teenage reasoning. Advancing to regional or state competitions meant traveling to big cities, staying in hotels, eating good food, and missing school for the events. At the time, that sounded like a pretty good deal.

I decided to do better.

In many ways, it worked in my favor. Although some people still whispered about the incident from seventh grade, or what they thought my father was doing to me, I was beginning to build a different reputation through sports and academics.

Still, every now and then, someone would approach me with comments about my past or speculate about my home life.

By that point, my father had conditioned me well. I had learned how to respond. If someone asked questions, I could quickly offer a believable answer and move the conversation somewhere else. It didn't mean shame wasn't speaking, but I couldn't let others know their words were piercing my soul.

Around that same time, I began spending more time with some of my father's other children. At first, it felt awkward. They were older than me, and I didn't know exactly where I fit.

Eventually, I began to look up to two of them in particular. They were close enough in age that I wanted to spend time with them and learn from them.

Through those connections, I also discovered that I had more nieces, nephews, and siblings than I had previously known about.

Holidays were often the only time I saw many of them. Those gatherings could feel uncomfortable. Part of me always wondered what they knew—or what they suspected.

Did they know what our father was doing to me?

Did his former wife resent my presence because I was the child born from my father's relationship with my mother while he was still married to her?

Those were heavy questions for a young mind to carry.

At one point, one of my older sisters spoke honestly with me. She told me that welcoming me into the family had been difficult at first. To her, I represented the broken promises my father had made to her mother and the vows he had not kept.

Even though I had nothing to do with those choices, I listened. I didn't fully understand the depth of her feelings at the time, but I could see that the situation had caused pain for more than just me.

Over time, I learned how to exist between two different worlds— my life with my mother and siblings, and my connection to my father's extended family.

I still lived primarily with my mother, but my father increasingly wanted me present in his life outside of school hours. If he went somewhere, there was a good chance I was expected to be there too.

I managed to function well enough for family and others to believe I was okay, while the version of me who was carrying things no one could see was starting to feel the pressure of it all.

My mother's house became the place where I ate and slept, but much of my time revolved around him.

The live-in girlfriend my father had when the abuse first began was no longer around. In her place came other women, many of them young adults.

Watching those relationships was confusing. My father was abusing me while also maintaining relationships with these women. He told me God would not be pleased if I did such things, but I guess God had not spoken to him about his own sins.

At one point, I believe one of them began to suspect that something was wrong. Instead of trying to help me, however, she seemed to become jealous.

For weeks, she taunted me with comments and insults. At the store. At my father's house. I wanted to respond, but my father made it clear that I was not allowed to say anything to her, no matter what she said.

And then, when I was fourteen years old, the situation escalated, and she attacked me while I was at my father's house. Thankfully,

I had already assumed she would try something, so I was able to defend myself. Processing what had happened in that moment would take some time.

I was already trying to survive one situation, and now I was being pulled into another. Physically, there were minimal signs of an attack, but mentally, I couldn't believe this was my life.

How did following all the rules set before me by my father put me in such a position? I was confused, angry that my father hadn't stopped this before it escalated to this point, and even with all of this, I still had to brush it off and return to my mom's house as if nothing had happened. I couldn't tell her what happened because I didn't know how to tell her I'd been attacked by a woman trying to establish dominance as the top woman in my father's life.

This woman believed I was somehow standing in the way of her relationship with my father. If only she'd known he was using her, too.

By this point, my life felt like something out of a movie. Yet every day, I still had to show up at school, church, family gatherings, and both of my parents' homes as if everything were normal.

And in many ways, that chaos had become my normal. My life had been many things, excluding normal, for years, so whatever this was seemed fine.

With nowhere to turn and nobody to talk to, I kept moving forward. Things would happen, and I would be expected to move on as if nothing had happened.

Freedom, as I understood it then, would not come until I turned seventeen. At fourteen, that meant I still had about three years ahead of me.

Seventeen felt like a lifetime away.

Instead of dwelling on what I was going through, I focused on surviving those years the best way I could. I learned to endure. I learned to keep functioning.

And somehow, in the middle of all that confusion, pain, and abuse I was made to believe was God's plan, the coming years would still hold some of the most memorable parts of my teenage life—not because of the abuse, but because moments of relief and growth began to appear alongside the hardship.

Looking back now, I sometimes believe those moments were small reminders that even in the middle of broken circumstances, God had not forgotten me.

CHAPTER 5

Learning to Survive

By the start of ninth grade, so much had already transpired.

My brother, Dedrick, had passed away, and I watched my mother grieve the loss of her firstborn child. I had settled into the role my father insisted was God's plan for my life. I was helping raise my nephew, becoming more distant from my two remaining siblings in my mother's home, excelling in sports and academics, and growing closer to two of my siblings on my father's side.

At school, I had become the kind of student teachers appreciated—a Bible-carrying, rule-following, high-achiever. I was the type of student who sat in the front of the classroom, completed every assignment, and worked hard to meet expectations.

In many ways, though I was mentally stretched trying to keep track of all expectations in my normal day-to-day, as well as what my father required, I had learned to balance my double life well.

Around that same time, I began making real friends. My guidance counselor told me about a summer engineering program at Mississippi State University, and I attended before the school year began. That is where I met Jas.

Jas would become one of my closest friends throughout high school. We also met another girl during the program, and the three of us quickly formed a bond. Before the program ended, we made a promise to each other that one day we would all attend Mississippi State together.

Life, of course, would unfold differently over time, but in that moment, the idea felt wonderful. For one of the first times in a long while, I felt accepted and connected.

That feeling stood out to me because it was so different from what I was used to. It felt easy, normal even.

I didn't realize how much I needed it until I experienced it.

High school came with its own set of challenges.

Although the bullying had mostly stopped, the damage it had done remained. I still struggled with feelings of not being good enough—not pretty enough, not worthy enough, not the type of girl that boys wanted to pursue. Years of emotional abuse had quietly shaped the way I saw myself. And it didn't help that any time I liked a guy, my father had a reason for why it wouldn't work.

So I focused on what I knew how to control: sports and academics.

I continued to excel in the classroom and on the track field. Winning medals became somewhat routine—gold, silver, and bronze at regional and state competitions. Track gave me structure, discipline, and something positive to work toward. I also had an amazing coach who believed in me.

Sports also gave me friendships.

Most of the girls I grew close to on the team were one year ahead of me, but we depended on each other. On the relay team, success required trust. Each runner relied on the next to finish the race strong.

But even those friendships had limits.

Although we were close as teammates, I was rarely allowed to spend time with them outside of school or practice. Whenever I wanted to hang out with friends, my father seemed to have a reason why I shouldn't.

Sometimes it was a dream he claimed to have had.
Other times, it was a vision or a warning he said God had given him.

Looking back now, it may sound unbelievable. But at the time, fear had already settled deep inside me. I believed what he said, and I was too afraid to test whether it was true.

Most nights during that time, the closest thing I had to normal teenage interaction was talking on the phone with Jas. We didn't attend the same school, so we rarely saw each other in person, but our conversations meant a lot to me.

Eventually, though, my father seemed to sense that our friendship was becoming important to me. Isolation had always strengthened his control over my life.

Slowly, he began planting doubts in my mind about Jas. Small comments, subtle accusations, and quiet warnings brought a shift in how I saw her and began to make the friendship harder to maintain. Over time, the doubts created distance where there had once been connection, and the relationship faded.

It didn't disappear completely, but it weakened. Years would pass before we would reconnect in the way we once had.

By then, I had already learned a painful pattern: when my father decided that something—or someone—was becoming important to me, they often disappeared from my life.

It took years before I understood that isolation was one of the tools he used to keep me under his control.

Still, I kept moving forward.

By the time I reached tenth grade, I began meeting nice boys at school. I found myself wanting what many other teenagers had—a simple relationship with someone my own age. I wanted someone to see me for who I was, or at least the version I could show them, not through the lens of rumors or my past.

But there was a problem.

My father made it very clear that I was not allowed to date. He was not shy about telling others this either.

Around that same time, his behavior began changing in other ways. He became more emotionally and verbally abusive, and he had also developed a strong interest in gambling.

Many nights, I found myself accompanying him to the casino. Sometimes I went inside with him if I could sneak past security. Other times, I sat alone in the car and waited while he gambled.

I realize, now, how dangerous those situations could have been. There were nights when I sat alone in that car until one or two in the morning simply because I was too young to go in, but he still needed to know where I was and that I was under his control.

Eventually, exhaustion began to set in.

And sitting in the dark, waiting, gave me a lot of time to think. And most of those thoughts led back to the same question:

Is this what my life is supposed to be?

There were many nights when I cried quietly to myself. I often wrote about wanting something very simple: a normal father–daughter relationship.

The pages of my journal became one of the only places where I could be honest without fear.

Sometimes during the drives home from the casino, I would write in the dark. I couldn't see the page clearly, but I knew what I was writing. The words were familiar by then.

Even if no one else saw those words, they were real in a way my spoken words couldn't be.

I had even tried mentioning the idea of "normal" to him once. The conversation did not go well.

His response always circled back to the same phrase: "A man takes care of one woman."

Apparently, in his interpretation of the world, daughters were not included in that category.

I felt discouraged, but then I remembered the covenant he had forced me into at thirteen.

Seventeen.

That was the number I held onto.

It gave me something to look forward to. Even in uncertainty, that number felt like a promise.

If his words were true, then once I reached seventeen, I would finally be free. The seven years of control would end, and I could begin living a normal life.

The closer I got to my seventeenth birthday, the more hopeful I became. I imagined what freedom might feel like. I imagined making my own decisions and living like the other teenagers around me, even having a boyfriend.

For the first time in years, I allowed myself to look forward to the future.

I truly believed freedom was coming.

That things would change, and I would get a chance to live my life on my terms.

But as I would soon learn, people who thrive on control rarely give it up willingly.

Part 3

Living Under Control

CHAPTER 6

Freedom Denied

I started planning for my freedom.

Seventeen was coming, and I was planning to hold my father to his word.

After all, your word is your bond, right?

This wasn't just about a birthday. It felt like everything I had dealt with was finally coming to an end.

As my seventeenth birthday drew near, I reminded him of what he had said. He had been the one to say, "until 17." I told him I wanted to go free and live my life.

Saying those words out loud felt bigger than I expected.

It was the first time I had clearly expressed what I wanted for myself.

I wanted to date and just be. I wanted to make my own decisions and not be bound to my father and his way of living.

I didn't want to be his wife anymore. I was tired.

This wasn't a thought that had just popped into my head. It was a truth that had been building quietly over time, growing stronger each time something felt off.

The closer I got to seventeen, the more I started noticing things that I would now classify as gaslighting, but back then, I had no language for it. Everything I did on my own was wrong, so I learned to second-guess myself often. Even the smallest decisions could turn into proof that I couldn't be trusted to think for myself.

Now, when I say everything I did on my own was wrong, I do not mean that it was actually wrong. I mean, my father made me feel like I didn't know how to make good decisions. I didn't know what was best for me. God was speaking to him for me, and that was what was good. If what I thought or what I decided didn't line up with what he said God told him, showed him, or gave to him in a vision, then it wasn't right.

Then seventeen came, and I was so excited.

The moment I had been waiting for was finally here, and for a moment, I allowed myself to believe everything was about to change.

But the excitement was short-lived.

My father must have thought I wasn't serious about wanting the abuse to stop. To say he was shocked would be an understatement.

He gave me every negative reason why I shouldn't be without him in this covenant. Then, when I persisted, he gave an angry okay. But anger quickly moved to action.

Feeling uneasy, I left my father's house, driving away in my mother's green Toyota Camry.

I drove toward my mom's house, about a fifteen-minute drive away. To my surprise, he followed me. I stopped at the local post office, and he stopped too.

Why hadn't I just kept going and driven straight to my mom's house?

Then action moved to words. Words that cut into an already broken girl's very lacking self-esteem.

He got out of his vehicle and began questioning my reasoning for wanting to end things, as if what was happening was a consensual dating relationship.

He accused me of wanting to break free so I could freely have sex with others. He told me I would just be a slut and that no one would want me. He made me feel lower than low, as if that were even possible at the time.

The way he spoke made me feel like I had done something wrong just by wanting my own life.

That was the day I realized he never intended for me to have hope, or any real chance of true escape.

I would have to endure until he said I could go free.

Years later, I would realize that what he was doing in that post office parking lot was a scare tactic. He wanted me to believe he was the only one who would ever have me. But at the time, and according to him, I could have anyone I wanted when the time was right. Right now, though, God had only ordained him for me.

So the abuse continued.

And a new rule was activated:

Finish college, then freedom.

That meant another potentially five to seven years of this life as my normal.

Deep down, I started to question whether that timeline would keep moving.

And in that moment, I began to understand something I hadn't fully understood before:

Freedom from him wouldn't be free or easy.

CHAPTER 7

Dreams Denied

Beat down by the verbal abuse and silenced by my father's control, I accepted this new timeline as fact.

It wasn't that I agreed with it, but I didn't see another option.

It is amazing how powerful the brain is even in protection mode. It was as if the situation flipped a safety switch, and survival was the new name of the game.

I stopped focusing on what I wanted and started focusing on what would keep things from getting worse.

I continued to excel in sports and academics, so much so that at the end of my track season, junior year of high school, colleges were taking notice.

Now, in years past, I had seen scouts come to look at other people, but me?

And after all, Marion Jones had been the track star I admired when I was young, and I was determined to make it to the Olympics as a sprinter.

I was going places.

I knew it.

I'll never forget the day I realized how close that dream was.

I was sitting in science class when there was a knock at the door. Coach G was looking for me. As soon as I walked out of the classroom, she was grinning big and handing me a large packet from Ole Miss.

And like the scene in *Love and Basketball* when Quincy reads the words from Monica's college acceptance letter, my coach said, "They want you."

Instant excitement.

I was so ecstatic. My hard work was paying off. I couldn't account for what was happening in my personal life at home, but this, this was mine. This belonged to me.

This was also the year I went to state in cross country and track and came home with gold.

It felt like proof that my life could be something different, bigger than what I had been experiencing.

So, I enjoyed that moment and allowed everything else to fade into the background.

I celebrated it with my coach. I went back into class joyful and hopeful, realizing just how close my dreams of becoming an Olympian were.

Unfortunately, it was short-lived.

When I shared the excitement with my father, he didn't have the same reaction I had.

I don't know why I thought to expect support or congratulatory words from him.

Even though the opportunity would still be a year away, because I had to finish my senior year of high school first, my father convinced me to give up cross country for my senior year.

That meant less prep for spring track.

At the time, it didn't feel like I had a real choice. It felt like something I had to agree to, even though I didn't fully understand what I was giving up.

I was still good, but my performance wavered in my senior year.

And unfortunately, that offer from Ole Miss went away.

My father knew a scholarship to Ole Miss meant obligations I wouldn't be able to get out of and, more importantly for him, it meant him losing his grip on controlling me. And he couldn't accept that.

I was devastated.

My father was elated.

The same moment that brought me sorrow brought him peace.

But there was still a little bit of hope.

My coach had another school looking at me, and they wanted to do an interview. I still remember talking to my father about this one. His response, because he was still against it, was simple:

"Take the interview. But decline the offer."

Taking that offer would have meant I would be about four hours away and really out of his control, and again, something he wasn't willing to allow.

So, at his command, I went through the interview process, and when the scholarship offer came, I declined.

Just like that, something I had worked toward for years was gone.

And I didn't fully realize it at the time, but it wasn't just an opportunity lost.

Dreams of the Olympics were now a thing of the past.

A dream I had carried for years ended quietly in that moment.

Not because I wasn't capable, but because I wasn't free.

Years later, I would see an Olympic athlete—someone who competed in Mississippi at the same time I did, someone I knew of during my running years—and I couldn't help but think about the opportunity I was robbed of having.

As if that wasn't enough, I then had to tell Jas that I would not be attending Mississippi State University with her. I wasn't extremely sad about it because I had already realized that, though cool for the summer camp we attended, engineering was not my desired major or career path.

What I couldn't tell her was that it was also a no because my father didn't want me too far from his reach.

She didn't know about my secret torture, so telling her my father had said no had the potential to open a door of questions I wasn't ready or able to walk through.

CHAPTER 8

A Life Divided

High school graduation came and went, and college was next. I still ended up choosing Ole Miss on an academic scholarship, and my father was okay with it because I wouldn't have any extracurricular obligations that would keep me from him.

When I initially started, I met people but didn't really connect very much.

I was living a double life. One version of me existed with friends and classmates, and another existed with my father. After a while, it became exhausting trying to remember which stories and conversations belonged to which version of my life. What I said at school couldn't be what I said at home, and what I lived at home could never be shared at school. Living like that for years meant constantly thinking two steps ahead, always careful not to let the wrong version of my life slip into the wrong conversation.

I was excited, though, because I was attending the same college some of my siblings on my father's side had attended, and two of them, the two I felt closest to at the time, still lived close by.

I thought it was going to be great.

But then came more rules from my father.

Come home on the weekends, or whenever I tell you to.
Answer your phone always.
Boys only want one thing, no matter what they tell you, so don't date.

Those weren't suggestions.

They were expectations that were to be followed.

And if I did like someone and told my father about it, he would suddenly have a vision or a dream from God, or he would just know that it would end badly for me if I didn't forget about the person.

College was not what I thought it would be.

It looked like freedom from the outside, but internally, I still felt controlled.

No other students I met had these types of rules. They were happy and living and seemed normal, more normal than me anyway. I was getting stress from all sides, living a double life, wanting to be an adult, and feeling like a puppet being controlled by the puppeteer.

My grades began to drop, and I wasn't motivated. I had also chosen a major that had been chosen for me.

Living a double life in college proved harder than in high school.

It was harder to explain why I had to go home every weekend or why I couldn't go some of the places or do some of the things the other young adults my age were doing.

Emotionally and mentally, I was overwhelmed, and my grades dropped.

I was on scholarship and would go on probation if I couldn't get my grades up, which meant I risked losing school altogether.

Instead of staying and trying to bring my grades up, I transferred to a community college, much to my father's happiness.

Attending the community college meant I would commute back and forth daily instead of only on weekends. This gave my father more access and the ability to control more of my movements.

He was happy to feel more in control.

I was happy he wasn't stressing me out as much.

This arrangement worked for about a semester.

I started a work-study position on campus and made a friend, Tracey, who would, in the future, become like a sister to me and accept the role of godmother to my children.

I also met a guy who seemed nice and respectful. I decided I would give it a shot, but there were no attachments and no labels, so it felt safer. That made it less likely that my father would find a reason to make me stop talking to someone.

So, we talked.

Even in something that should have felt normal, like talking to a boy, I was still hesitant.

I didn't know how to fully show up without fear or the constant internal what-ifs.

As time went on and the semester ended, I decided that when the fall semester came, I would stay on campus.

It was great.

A little bit of freedom.

My father didn't protest too much because there was still the understanding that I would come home if he needed me to come home.

I started making friends and hanging out more, and I changed my major to English, which was something I really wanted to do.

I didn't fully realize it yet, but things were shifting.

Some things were great.

Some things were not.

Remember the guy I was talking to… we never put a label on anything, never made it official, but it felt real. And it wasn't sexual. Then I found out he was talking to other girls too.

I was crushed.

There was an entire scene, an entire process, and looking back, I'm like, oh my gosh, all the things that happened.

I tried to move on, but I was also hurt. I was embarrassed. And once again, the roots of *you're not good enough, pretty enough, worthy enough* grew deeper.

Then there was another guy.

I met him at a little function, and we hit it off. I told my father I wanted to go out with him, and his response was:

"Not in a car I paid for."

So, what did I do?

I bought the car from my father.

Yep, you read that right.

What father does that?

Obviously, the kind who sees himself as your husband and controller and not your father.

It felt like I was buying a small piece of my independence.

Then, I went on the date.

That one date was all it would be. This crush was short-lived and again, non-sexual. My father had instilled in me this fear that God would only be pleased with what my father was doing to me, and if I attempted to do anything similar with someone else, I would be in danger of hellfire.

So that fear, although twisted, kept me from doing a lot of things in college that some of my peers were doing.

My father was happy that the date didn't turn into more, and his attitude shifted once he realized it was over.

Around that same time, I ended up joining a singing group on campus. We formed a choir and traveled singing praise songs, and one of the guys in the group was actually a minister who would also preach at these events.

It was amazing.

I was connecting with people, albeit still living a double life, but I was able to have fun and be around people who accepted me—or at least the version of me I showed them—without judgment.

It was also one of the first times I had to deal with true tension in friendly relationships, and since I hadn't had the best practice with that, it came with challenges. I had to learn that hearing the hard truth and being held accountable in love was not the same as the evil-intended and manipulative words my father would say to me.

Though the group would only last about a year, it really taught me quite a bit about commitment and friendship, even though I couldn't share the real me with them.

It was also during that season that I realized my relationship with God was broken.

I felt Him, but I also felt disconnected from Him. I had given my life to God years ago, at my father's church, but did I really know what it meant?

I would later learn that a lot of that was tied to my view of my father and how that intertwined with my view of our Heavenly Father.

But back to the community college days.

I finished my time there, and then I transferred back to Ole Miss so I could finish out my degree in English and become a teacher.

Tracey had already transferred there, so I knew I was starting with at least one friend.

My goal was simple: focus on school and work, then graduate.

Then I got a job and met a boy. By now, at age 20, I felt I could choose to have a boyfriend if I wanted to.

And for the first time in about six years, I let my guard down.

And I was so afraid.

I was afraid I had disappointed God and put myself in danger of hellfire, and I was afraid of my father's reaction.

I don't know which one I feared more, but I was definitely afraid in both scenarios.

That relationship was short-lived, but it truly impacted my life.

Silenced No More

For the first time in years, I found myself at a place where I was tired of holding the secret of what was going on in my life, and I almost told this guy.

But I didn't.

I can remember it like it was yesterday.

I was on the phone with this guy, while at my mother's house, and it was like I felt the urge to tell him, but the words wouldn't come out.

So the abuse continued.

And so did my silence.

By now, the new school year was starting, the fall semester of my junior year, and I got an apartment close to campus and close to my job.

Independence loading, faulty foundation crashing.

I still had to go home often enough, but I had my own place to retreat to.

Then came a reality check, but not in the way you might think.

The semester had been going for about a month or so, and it was a typical weekend. I had finished up in my apartment, finished up at school, and was preparing to head home for the weekend.

As I was leaving my apartment complex and getting onto the highway, I was hit and run off the road by what was believed to be a reckless driver.

It was a hit-and-run.

As I spun out of control and off the road, I just remember calling on Jesus.

In that moment, nothing else mattered.

Not control. Not fear. Just survival.

The car finally stopped, thanks to a tree.

I was able to climb out of my car and make my way up to the road. Someone had seen it happen and came to check on me. Apparently, the same person who ran me off the road had almost hit someone else, too.

I was so distraught about my car, but when the police officers arrived, there was one in particular who helped put things into perspective for me.

"Ma'am, your car stopped by a tree, but below that tree was a drop-off. You can get another car, but not another life."

Though still sad about the car, I was thankful God had saved me, even if my car was totaled.

I went home that weekend shaken up, but thankful.

When I returned to school the next week, I was determined to get serious about God again.

Not the version I had been taught through control, but the version I would need to discover for myself.

I went to Bible study on campus, and wouldn't you know, there was this guy who saw that I didn't have my Bible and offered to share. We sat together, and I guess he forgot his pencil because he reached over without asking and borrowed mine.

But I didn't mind. This guy just so happened to be the same guy I'd met in 2005 when I was a freshman. I thought he was cute, but he was an upperclassman, and I didn't approach him back then. But I always remembered him.

After Bible study, we talked. Turns out, he was finishing up his last semester before graduating.

God's timing was perfect.

It felt like something new had the possibility to begin.

He shared about his poetry book, and I shared about the wreck I had just had. He gave me a copy of his book to take home and read. Eventually, I reached out to him on Facebook, and we began seeing each other at Bible studies and fellowship hangouts.

About a month later, he asked me out.

We really hit it off, and I was so excited.

But there was one problem.

Anyone I liked was a threat to my father, and I really liked this guy.

So, I did the only thing I could think of.

I hid my relationship from my father.

It felt wrong to hide something that felt right, but I had already learned that honesty didn't always lead to safety.

If my father invited himself to my apartment, I made sure Josh was not around. After all, he had his own apartment. I didn't talk about him around my father, and it went well for about two and a half months.

Then came January 2008.

I got sick and needed to go home to the family doctor, but I didn't want to make the almost hour-long drive by myself, so my boyfriend came with me.

Everything was going fine.

My mom met us at the doctor's office. The remedy was simple: a sinus cocktail shot to help alleviate the symptoms and rest.

We stopped by my mom's house before heading back toward campus.

But before we could leave, my father drove by. Seeing my car in the yard, he stopped.

He came in with a smile, but when he saw this guy sitting in the chair, the smile disappeared with quickness.

Josh tried to speak, but my father refused.

He didn't understand what was silently unfolding, but I knew I was in trouble.

Not because I had done something wrong, but because I knew how my father would see Josh…as a threat.

Silenced No More

My father walked out of the house and waited, and I knew he was waiting for me to come out.

So I did.

"Who is that?" he asked.

I calmly told him who Josh was.

"Are y'all sleeping together?"

It wasn't, "Are y'all dating?"
It wasn't, "Is he a nice guy?"
You know, the normal questions a parent might ask first.

His focus was on sex.

I lied.

"No, we're not."

I don't know that he believed me, but angrily, he left.

My boyfriend and I returned to campus. He went to his apartment, and I went to mine.

Later that week, we had plans to cook and eat in, but the power went out, so we opted to go out for pizza instead.

While sitting at the pizza place waiting for the pizza, I talked to my father on the phone.

I couldn't lie.

Even when I wanted to.

Fear had trained me to tell him the truth, even when it cost me.

That's the thing about being controlled by someone. Your life is not your own. And when you lie to them, you feel afraid they are going to find out anyway.

So, I told the truth.

"Yes, we have been having sex."

I didn't have to break up with him, but my father was angry and had new rules for me now.

"Whenever I call, you come to me or be ready for me to come to you."

I knew what that meant, and I agreed and got off the phone, knowing control would only get tighter.

I went back in to meet my Josh as if all was fine.

By this point, I knew how to be Erica the college student with Josh, and Erica the silent, submissive one, with my father.

Again, my brain and body were in survival mode, and this is how I maintained safety physically, emotionally, and mentally, or at least the best I could.

Things went on like this for about two months.

My father became more heartless. Maybe he had always been that way, but now that I wasn't around him twenty-four hours a day, I could actually see it for what it was, at least a little more clearly than before.

Part 4

The Beginning of Resistance

CHAPTER 9

The Moment Everything Shifted

Spring break 2008 came, and my father wanted me available, no questions asked.

Josh and I were on a bit of a break during this time, but we had still been seeing each other here and there.

I didn't know what was next, but I knew something had to change soon.

By now, my sister, Kita, had a three-year-old daughter whom I was quite fond of and tried to spend time with often. I went to pick up my niece so she could spend a weekend with me. As our normal routine, we went to Applebee's to eat. I ordered my usual, the boneless hot wings, but this time something was off.

The wings didn't taste right. While my niece enjoyed her meal, I was silently wondering what was going on.

That's strange, I thought.

That had never happened before.

And I had been eating those wings for years. As a college student, I looked forward to the boneless wings special on Wednesday nights in our college town.

When I took my niece home at the end of her stay, I stopped by the local Walmart and grabbed a pregnancy test.

The wings not tasting right still did not sit right with me.

The next morning, I took the test, not really sure what I was expecting.

But when it said pregnant, so many thoughts rushed through my mind at once.

What?

What do I do?

Do I keep the baby?

Not keeping it is not an option.

All of these questions and thoughts were running through my head about a mile a minute.

I gathered myself enough to find my phone, call Josh, and say, "I'm pregnant."

He was just as shocked as I was.

We had been on a break and had not been active for several weeks, so I was scared.

Then another thought came to my mind, one I didn't want to be true.

My father had never gotten me pregnant, but what if—

I didn't even want to finish that thought. The idea of that scared me more than anything else in that moment.

Reality was, I had to go home and ask my mom for my medical documents.

So, I did.

"Hey, Mom, can I have my birth certificate and Social Security card?"

"Huh?" was her response. "Why do you need those? The only reason you'd need those is if…"

And in that moment, I think she realized I was pregnant.

There was no hiding it.

"Yes, ma'am," was my response.

I was 21 at the time, and had never had a need to ask my mom for those, so she knew.

Now, mind you, my older sister was already pregnant with her second child at the time, so my mom was about to be welcoming two grandbabies months apart.

She gave me the documents, and I went to the health department. They confirmed that I was approximately two months pregnant.

Hearing it out loud made it real in a different way. It wasn't just a possibility and couldn't be chalked up to a faulty test. I was really pregnant.

And I still had to tell my father.

I was nervous, but I told him.

I didn't know how he was going to respond, but I knew this conversation would be different.

He said he needed to see for himself.

And he had his way of checking.

Why couldn't he just take my word and the word of the doctor? Why did violating me have to be his response?

It became clear that control had always been more important to him than anything else, even in a situation that should have been handled with care.

It was in that moment that I knew that would be the last time he would sexually abuse me.

Something rose up on the inside of me.

The "something" wasn't loud, and there wasn't this overwhelmingly courageous outcry in that moment.

But the feeling was strong enough for me to recognize that something had changed.

I had a baby to protect.

I couldn't quite put the psychological or even the everyday words fully to what had happened to me for over a decade, but I knew the baby growing inside of me deserved to be protected.

For the first time, my decisions weren't just about surviving. They were about protecting someone else from experiencing what I had lived through.

I prepared myself to tell my father no and not back down.

The next time he thought he was going to violate me, I told him I couldn't let that happen.

I was choosing to say no and sticking with it for the first time in over a decade.

I should not have been surprised at his response, but this was different.

I thought I had seen him angry before, but I was about to find out the levels he would go to.

Because control doesn't let go without a fight.

CHAPTER 10

The Cost of Saying No

Refusing to be abused was one of the hardest things I've done in my life.

It was one thing to say "no more."
It was another thing entirely to walk that out.

For years, I had been used to doing what others told me to. Standing on my own and meaning it required a kind of strength I wasn't sure I had yet.

At first, my father didn't believe I was serious. Eventually, after some words I will not repeat in these pages, he got the message. Even so, he was angry and relentless.

Because I was still afraid of my father, I tried to avoid him. That was hard when he would come to my mom's house unannounced just to say "hi."

I was free physically now.

So why couldn't I just tell somebody what he had been doing to me for all those years?

In June of 2008, I was about four months pregnant. I had just lost my job. My boyfriend had gone away for military training, and I could no longer afford to pay my rent or my car payment. I didn't want to ask Josh for help because that might mean sharing what I had kept secret for so long.

I asked my mom for help, and she stepped in without hesitation. She paid the last payment on my apartment, and I moved back in with her.

Because I was no longer under my father's control, he refused to help me financially.

No longer able to pay for my car, I wanted to sell it to Kita, but my father thought that was a bad idea and wouldn't allow it. Instead, he agreed to buy it from me. Even though the physical abuse had ended, he was still controlling aspects of my life, and I didn't even realize it.

Family members on my father's side, only hearing what he was sharing with them, seemed to look down on me. I was pregnant, still in college, unmarried—what many people would call "out of order."

One of them actually called me, out of the blue, and it was clear they wanted me to admit that I was pregnant.

By that time, I felt alone and was mentally struggling just to keep it together. The reality of what I had endured for all those years began hitting me all at once, like a ton of bricks.

I wasn't sure how I was going to survive the aftermath.

And I knew I needed to tell my boyfriend the truth.

One night, I drove to a local diner and parked my car.

I sat there for a moment before calling him.

I dialed his number and waited for him to pick up. After the initial check-in, I said, "I have something to tell you."

I was nervous, unsure of how he'd respond, but I was also afraid, felt alone, and could no longer carry the secret that felt like it was trying to kill me.

I began telling him what I had endured for the past eleven years.

The words felt heavy coming out of my mouth, like I was finally saying out loud what I had spent years pretending wasn't happening. I couldn't believe I was actually sharing the secret I had been taught for so long to keep.

In that moment, I was freeing myself, even if I didn't fully realize it yet.

I told him that I understood if he wanted to back out. I told him I wouldn't keep him from his child. I didn't want him to feel obligated to endure this reality with me.

Silenced No More

He could have taken the out.

Much to my surprise, he responded with three simple words:

"I love you."

For the first time, someone knew the truth and didn't turn away.

Instead, he chose to stay.

I was scared, but I also felt a strange sense of relief.

I tried to keep moving forward. I was still in school. Josh and I were trying to figure things out, and somehow, I was trying to hold out hope that things would be okay.

Since my father had agreed to buy my car from me, he went to the bank because he knew the banker and worked out some type of arrangement.

Before turning the car in, I made one more decision.

I drove the car to visit Josh while he was away for military training out of state. My father was not pleased that I took the car on a trip when I was supposed to be turning it in, but I needed to see Josh first, the only person I felt I had in my corner, the only person who knew of the abuse I had endured.

While I was there, my boyfriend got a glimpse of my father's anger.

My father called repeatedly, but I didn't answer.

He left a voicemail saying all kinds of ungodly things.

Josh encouraged me to ignore the negativity and enjoy the time we had together. I tried to do exactly that, because honestly, I didn't know what life would look like when I returned to Mississippi.

Nothing could have prepared me for what breaking free would actually mean.

When I returned to Mississippi, I was told to turn the car in, sign a document at the bank, and that would be that. After all, I was just his daughter now. But, I didn't feel like his daughter. I felt lost.

To make matters worse, he told the local banker that I wasn't trustworthy. When I went to speak with the banker myself, he told me he didn't want my business and didn't want anything to do with me.

He didn't know me.

He didn't know my story.

Yet, he had already decided who I was.

If only he had known the truth, maybe he wouldn't have made me feel like doing the right thing—putting a stop to the abuse and standing up for myself—was somehow wrong.

Part 5

Breaking What Held Me

CHAPTER 11

The First Real Break

Things didn't change all at once, but my father's control wasn't the driving force in my life like before.

Fear, though still present, didn't run every waking hour of my life.

With Josh away for training, I needed someone to talk to.

I turned to Lena. I first met her at the job I had just been let go from.

She was a mom of two. She loved Jesus deeply. And she was the kind of person who would lovingly tell you the truth.

While on the job, Lena quickly became like a big sister to me. For almost a year, she was my mentor, making sure I knew what to do and how to improve where needed to be successful.

Even though I was no longer working with the company, I would still stop by and talk to Lena.

On one of those occasions, I finally told her about the molestation and the pregnancy.

There was compassion.

There was concern.

There was no judgment.

She invited me to stay with her for a weekend, and that weekend turned into several visits throughout the summer.

While I stayed with her, we went to her church, spent time with her family, and her children welcomed me as if I were part of their family, too.

On one particular visit, we went to her church during what I believe was a revival service.

There was a prophetess there that night.

I don't remember her name, but I remember that she saw me.

Not just the pregnant girl sitting in the crowd.

She saw the real me.

The broken me.
The abused me.

She called me forward and spoke about the pain I had been carrying. She encouraged the men in the church to show me what real fathers were meant to look like.

At the time, I didn't fully understand what she meant.

But I cried.

There was prayer.

There was a sense of release.

That night, when I returned to Lena's house, I slept with a level of peace I hadn't felt in a long time.

If only healing had been as simple as that.

Life moved forward, but the weight of what had happened still followed me.

For the next five months, my life was busy: doctor's appointments to check on my growing baby, summer courses, and then fall classes for my senior year. My plan was clear. I would have my baby at the end of that semester, return in the spring, finish my final classes, and graduate.

My support system consisted of my mom, my sister Kita, and my dear friend Tracey. I eventually asked Tracey if she would be the godmother to my unborn child. Josh was supportive too, but there was only so much he could do at the time. He was now on active duty in the military and stationed in another state.

As if the hormones from pregnancy weren't enough, I realized that although I was free physically from the sexual abuse, the mental and emotional effects still lingered.

On days when I was at my mom's house while she was at work, my father would occasionally show up. Sometimes I would look out the window, see his car in the driveway, and feel my stomach drop. I didn't know I had the option to say no to him coming into my mom's house.

Once inside, his words were emotionally abusive and mentally wounding. He tried to convince me that I was making a mistake by telling him no and by moving forward with my life.

When it came to my pregnancy, he even tried to suggest that there was a possibility the baby was his.

Surely that couldn't be true… right, God?

I was determined to stand my ground, and even still, his presence carried the same fear from all the years and months before.

The two people who knew about my tortured past were not close enough to come to my rescue. At this point, I had not told my mom anything, and I wasn't ready—or even sure I knew how—to have that conversation with her.

I was embarrassed that the abuse had gone on for so long, as if it were somehow my fault. Shame has a way of convincing victims that they should have done something differently, even when the truth is that the responsibility never belonged to them in the first place.

It would take years for me to understand that surviving something does not make you responsible for it.

The visits eventually decreased as he saw I would not be changing my mind. I also learned to stay away from the house when my mom wasn't home. If I couldn't keep him from coming over, I could go somewhere he wouldn't go.

So, if I wasn't in class or at my sister's house, I was probably somewhere by myself, trying to make it through each day.

Feeling safe enough to share, I confided in a family member on my mother's side. Their advice was simple: give it to God and live my life. I was trying to do that, but it wasn't that simple.

I was also asked a question that stayed with me:

If I couldn't tell him that I loved him, had I truly forgiven him?

It was up to me to make things right, even though all this wrong had been done to me for years???

Once again, someone else's words made me question whether I deserved to suffer while others walked away from what they had done.

"Let go. Let God. Get over it."

Those words would become a recurring theme I would hear over the years.

A theme that made me question my Christianity and even my salvation.

But it was also a theme that stirred anger in me toward family members who could not seem to understand that I was the victim.

Those words were often spoken with good intentions, but to me, they felt like instructions to skip over the pain instead of healing from it.

Despite everything, I worked hard to stay focused on my courses and on bringing a healthy baby into the world.

Even though Josh was stationed away on duty, he made it a priority to travel from Georgia to Mississippi every month to see me and talk to our unborn child.

He would place his hand on my stomach and talk to the baby as if our child could already hear him.

I was always excited when Josh came for a visit and sad to the point of tears when he would leave.

Those visits reminded me that even in a difficult season, there was still one person in my life who cared about me and the life growing inside of me.

In those moments, I felt a kind of peace that reminded me that life was still moving forward.

CHAPTER 12

Motherhood and Movement

Months came and went. There was a baby shower surrounded by loving people, and then it was finally time to give birth to my baby girl.

Josh drove in from Georgia to be there. I was nervous but excited. My mom and Tracey would also join me in the delivery room.

Labor was long, and the pain was intense. After an epidural, I took a nap. After about twelve hours, it seemed my daughter was not in a rush to make her entrance into the world. It was getting late, and Tracey had to leave. Josh was napping on and off, and my mom was excitedly and expectantly waiting.

A few hours later, it was finally time to push.

With Josh and my mom by my side, our daughter made her grand entrance in the early morning hours.

Though unsure of what parenthood would look like, we were there now, so we would figure it out.

Josh happily cut the umbilical cord, and my mom was beaming with joy over her newest grandbaby—a healthy, beautiful baby girl.

Later that day, my big sister and her family arrived for a visit. Throughout the day, other family members and friends came to see us, but what I wasn't expecting was for my father to show up in my delivery room.

Who told him I was there?
Why did he feel he had the right to be there?

I didn't want him there.

There were multiple people in the room, and neither my boyfriend nor I knew what to say in the moment. Thankfully, his visit was short, and I don't recall him saying many words.

Even in the so-called freedom from his physical grip, he still seemed to think he could do as he pleased without fear of anyone saying or doing anything to him.

Maybe he knew I was still afraid of him. I knew I was.

And he certainly didn't know the fullness of what Josh knew about him.

Either way, I had no plan for my father to be around my daughter. I had to protect her. I knew what he was capable of, and I was willing to do whatever I had to in order to keep him from her.

Holding my daughter in my arms awakened something in me I had never felt before. I could not change what had happened to me, but I could make sure it never happened to her.

After we were released from the hospital, Josh was able to spend a few extra days with us before returning to his duty station. To my surprise, he made sure not to leave for Georgia before proposing to me first.

He had talked to his pastor at church and told him about this girl—me—whom he loved. He explained that I had been abused in my childhood and that he wanted to know how to love me well.

I was taken aback that he had the wisdom and desire to seek counsel so he could learn how to love someone carrying such deep wounds. He had never dealt with anything like this before, yet he still wanted to learn.

That was proof that my father's words weren't all true.

Someone *did* want to be with me.
Someone *did* love me.

I wasn't damaged goods.

Of course, I said yes.

We enjoyed the moment, and then Josh returned to Georgia for the next month while I adjusted to mom life.

After about a week, I had to return to campus to finish up the semester. My professors were very understanding and worked with me so I could complete my assignments. I was grateful.

Mom life on top of a seven-course college load was more challenging than I realized it would be.

My mom was truly a gift during this season. Not only had she helped purchase things for my daughter, but she also changed her work schedule so she could be home with the baby during the day while I attended class.

She wanted me to succeed and made sacrifices for me that, at the time, allowed me to see the loving mom and grandmother she truly was.

Since I gave birth just before Thanksgiving, I was thankful that Christmas break was around the corner. I would have about six weeks to rest and spend time with my little one.

To make matters even better, Josh was driving down from Georgia to take us back with him for four weeks.

I was beaming with excitement.

I had only been to Georgia once before, so this would be an adventure.

While there, I was able to attend my fiancé's church and meet the pastor who had given him such wise advice about how to love a broken woman.

The church felt real. The people were welcoming, and I knew that when I moved there, this would be my church too.

But I didn't want to wait until I moved there to make things right.

On New Year's Eve, we went to that same church, and both rededicated our lives to God. I was ready to do things right with the God I wanted a closer relationship with.

I think I was trying to get as far away as possible from what I had known all those years before and step into something real.

The new year came, and it was time to head back to Mississippi to finish my last semester of undergrad.

I was sad when Josh left to return to Georgia, but this time it was different.

I knew it was only temporary.

He was coming back for our daughter and me.

The next few months, life consisted of a full course load, a growing baby, a supportive mom, and once-a-month visits with Josh when he would make his way to Mississippi—except for the month of March.

We had been planning a summer wedding but realized we didn't want to wait.

During my spring break, I drove back to Georgia, and we got married.

There was no initial honeymoon, but for me, Josh was my knight in shining armor who was taking me away from all the bad I had experienced in Mississippi.

And that was better than a honeymoon.

After only a few days, I returned to Mississippi because graduation was still about two months away.

My mom was happy for me. I was planning to move as soon as I graduated. It would be bittersweet because my mom had grown attached to us being there.

But I knew I couldn't stay in that state any longer than I had to.

Too many memories of the unspeakable things I had endured lived there, and I couldn't stay there with them.

As the semester went on, I continued to focus on school, protecting my daughter, and preparing for the move.

Before graduation, my husband drove up to celebrate with my family and me.

Graduation day came on a Saturday, and true to my word, I was packed up and ready to go that Sunday.

It was emotional leaving home because my mom's house was what I knew.

But I also knew more was waiting for me.

And more than anything, I knew I was taking my daughter somewhere my father could not get to her.

CHAPTER 13

Learning to Stand Anyway

When I say I moved away and left everything behind—and almost everyone—I meant it. With the exception of a few, you would have thought I didn't really know that many people.

In all honesty, it wasn't that difficult to do. Growing up in the midst of the abuse, I had been isolated from family on my mother's side, so I never became very close to many of my cousins, with the exception of one. She is like a sister to me, even to this day.

So when I moved away, if it wasn't the people who grew up in my house, Tracey, or my cousin T, I probably didn't have much contact with them.

And it wasn't out of anger. It wasn't me trying to be mean.

Silenced No More

It was survival.

I was grown, but little Erica inside of me was still making sure we stayed safe, and survival mode was still activated.

I did keep in contact with my nieces because they were my big sister's girls, but I didn't keep in contact with my nephew—the one I had helped raise as a teenager.

Though I loved him, he was a constant reminder of what I had gone through all those years, and it was no fault of his own. He didn't know, or at least I didn't think he knew anything.

But I couldn't look at him without being reminded of his grandfather—my father.

So the easiest thing for me was to distance myself until there was no communication at all.

Years later, we would repair that distance, but at that time, he couldn't be a part of my life.

As we settled into living in Georgia, I experienced a different level of freedom. I wasn't looking over my shoulder or wondering if my father would knock on my door.

That fear was gone.

I lived. I enjoyed life. I raised my daughter with my husband.

We went to church. I got a job. Our daughter started daycare.

Life kept moving.

Things should have been fine, right?

But they weren't.

There was still so much healing that needed to happen.

Where I grew up, you didn't go talk to a therapist. You didn't air out your personal business or your family's problems.

You went to church.

And you gave it to Jesus.

So that's what I did again and again and again.

The number of times I went to the altar for prayer—asking God for healing, deliverance, the ability to forget the past, to forgive, and to move forward—is probably a number only Jesus knows.

Because even I lost count.

But even when I would go and experience a level of deliverance and healing, something still wasn't right.

I still didn't feel healed.

I still didn't feel fully free.

I was experiencing flashbacks and nightmares of the abuse. Insomnia was activated.

And those things were affecting my relationship with my husband and my ability to show up fully for my daughter.

But doing what I had been taught, I prayed about it, and I kept going.

Then we found ourselves pregnant again.

Unfortunately, that pregnancy was short-lived, and we experienced a miscarriage.

I was working, at the time, and tried to jump right back into work, but my body and emotions were not in agreement with that plan.

I wasn't able to focus at work the way I should have been, and it was impacting my performance. I spoke with my supervisor and was able to request a month-long time away to heal from the loss.

I am thankful for the supervisor and management who realized the importance of allowing me time to grieve the loss of our unborn child, realizing I needed to process the pain instead of rushing past the healing.

Within a few months, we found out we were pregnant again.

This time I was nervous and excited.

As time went on in that pregnancy, I began to feel the need to press charges against my father formally and officially as an adult, since the statute of limitations had not expired.

I talked to my husband, and he supported me.

I didn't know what the process would look like, but I wanted to try.

I didn't want it to be said that I didn't do enough—that I didn't do anything.

And I also didn't want someone else to be abused by my father because I stayed silent.

In preparation for pressing charges, I knew I would need to have a conversation with my mother.

So prayerfully, I did.

I didn't share all the graphic details, but I shared enough for her to know that her daughter had been abused by this man for over a decade.

That was a hard conversation.

But it was also a necessary one.

Understandably, there was a host of emotions, questions, and a moment between a mother and daughter that was long overdue.

And though I had been nervous before the conversation, I felt relief and fear released its grip just a little that day.

Next, I wanted to reach out to my siblings on my father's side—particularly the two older siblings I had grown close to during my teenage and college years, and another older sibling who had always been around.

All of them were my father's children.

I built up the courage to type a message.

Dear siblings,

I am planning to press charges against our father, and I wanted you to know beforehand.

For over a decade, he abused me, and I don't believe I am the only one.

I sent the message.

And it was like radio silence from two of the three.

One responded with a text message, but the response was not one I was ready—or willing—to receive. It didn't seem compassionate. It didn't seem caring.

"I'm sorry that happened to you, but…" I couldn't receive the rest of that message because I was frustrated and offended.

I thought at least one of them would call.
Even if they didn't know what to say.
Even if it was just silence on the other end of the phone.

But my phone never rang.

Not one of them asked questions.

Not one of them checked to see how I was doing.

And that hurt.

But life goes on, right?

And so, it did.

I continued forward with the process of pressing charges.

I reached out to CPS in a nearby town where I had grown up in Mississippi to track down records from when I was a little girl.

Unfortunately, the records weren't found.

They weren't there.

I also reached out to the police department.

Thankfully, in a small town, officers tend to stay around for many years. The same officer who took my statement when I was a little girl was still there.

Even so, I was only able to get so far.

But I wasn't ready to give up.

Then I decided to seek advice from someone I considered wise.

I shared my plan to press charges.

Their response surprised me—and once again made me question myself and my Christianity.

"He's still your father."

So now pressing charges would be wrong… because he was my father?

But he didn't seem to think too highly of being my father when he chose to violate me.

And now I was expected to be the bigger person.

What about standing up for myself meant I wasn't being a good Christian?

I was frustrated with the wisdom received. I felt like I was a little girl again, unsure if I'd done something wrong.

I began to wonder if I would be in the wrong if I proceeded with pressing charges.

Unsure of right and wrong in this situation, and with that "wisdom," I backed away.

Silenced No More

I even called my father and told him I had planned to press charges but had decided not to.

His response?

I shouldn't have been trying to do that anyway.

By then, he also knew that my husband knew the truth, and he felt I should never have told him either.

He had even confided in his sister—my aunt, someone I had once been fond of—and according to him, she also felt I should have stayed silent.

In what world was I the wrong one for speaking up about the wrong done to me?

I would never look at my aunt the same way again.

Since being a "good Christian" meant I should pray about it and still honor my father because the Bible said so, I was expected to move on.

If only it were that simple.

My siblings on my father's side still were not speaking to me.

I felt hurt.

I felt angry.

How could they not care?

Did they not believe me?

Was it too much for them to handle?

There were many days and nights when I questioned their silence.

Then my husband helped me shift my perspective.

"Babe, you spend all this time worrying and feeling sad about the people who don't want to be part of your life. Meanwhile, you have people who love you and want to spend time with you."

And he was right.

I couldn't make my siblings call me.

I couldn't make them message me back.

I couldn't make them choose a relationship with me.

I didn't know if what was broken between us would ever be fixed.

But I could love the people who were choosing to love me.

So instead of stressing over who left, I focused my attention on who was still there and made room for God to bring loving people into my life.

And, because healing is a journey, not a sprint, I knew I still had wounds from childhood trauma that needed attention.

I began searching for resources.

One of the most impactful was Joyce Meyer's *Battlefield of the Mind* and her sermons.

For the first time, I was hearing from someone who understood the sting of a father's ungodly touch.

For the first time, I realized that surviving something like this did not mean my life had to be defined by it.

She understood.

She had gone through what I had gone through.

And Joyce Meyer had found healing and become who God called her to be—with boldness and confidence.

I wanted that too.

God also connected me with a family at church who had experienced abuse at the hands of loved ones.

They shared their stories with me.

And for the first time, I felt safe enough to share mine.

Though the circumstances that connected us were painful, it was powerful to be around people who understood what I was walking through.

That was the beginning of real healing.

The beginning of moving forward.

CHAPTER 14

Letting Go Wasn't Easy

Time went on, and the sting of not having certain family members in my life began to hurt less and less.

That's not to say I didn't have emotional moments, but I was learning to focus more on the loved ones who remained in my life.

I was preparing for the birth of my second daughter, and things were moving along well. But another family shift was on the horizon. My husband got orders for an overseas move.

Wait. What?

The emotions that come with pregnancy while raising a toddler were already doing a number on me, but now I had to add in a massive move.

I had only lived in two places: Mississippi and Georgia. And now the military was sending us to Europe.

I didn't know if I could do that.

I knew I had been running from the pain of my past, but that just seemed too far away.

We had about five months to prepare for the move, but it still felt challenging to me. I had to call my mom to give her the news, and she was not excited about it either. She even offered to let me and the babies stay with her until my husband returned. But as tempting as the comfort of familiarity seemed, I knew staying behind while my husband moved abroad for almost four years would not be the right decision for me.

One saving grace was that we would have support because my husband's parents, who were prior military, still lived and worked in Europe. They would only be about two hours away from us. Though I had only seen them a few times in the two years I had been married to their son, I knew the support would be helpful as a mom of soon-to-be two little girls.

We continued preparing for the move while also preparing for the birth of our second daughter. I went in for a checkup about a week before my due date, and my blood pressure was elevated, so my doctor decided we would induce the very next morning.

By this time, I had become close with Mama V, a lady from our church, and her family. They made arrangements to keep my oldest, so Josh and I could focus on the arrival of baby girl number two.

The day of the induction started off like a regular day. I was given an epidural, and Josh and I settled in for what would be several hours of labor. I had been in communication with my mom, and though she wasn't there for the delivery, I knew I would see her after we were released from the hospital.

After about twelve hours of labor, my second daughter arrived at just under nine pounds, and there were complications shortly after. While everyone else was oohing and cooing over my baby girl, the doctors were trying to figure out why I was still bleeding. It went from celebration and congratulations to "Clear the room. Everybody out!" in a matter of seconds. Even my husband had to leave.

I hadn't even had a good look at my newest baby girl yet, and I wasn't given time to say anything to my husband.

In that moment, I didn't know if I would live or die, but I knew the doctors were doing everything they could. I said a prayer and believed that no matter what happened next, God was good.

I cry as I write this section because sometimes you do not realize the severity of what you have been through until you are on the other side, looking back at what God brought you out of.

Thankfully, God had a good, good plan, and I had a team of amazing doctors and nurses who worked to stop the bleeding. I do not remember everything, but I do remember injections, medicines, and resting. Once I was stabilized, they continued to monitor my levels and were prepared to give a blood transfusion if needed.

It was not necessary, and within a few days, I was released to go home with my baby.

I went home more grateful for life and for the family God had blessed me with.

Our oldest was now two, and she was adjusting to being a big sister and having to share her parents. And I, well, I was adjusting to so much at the time. I was coming to terms with giving up a job I thoroughly enjoyed because motherhood times two and an overseas move made it impossible to continue working there. I was still emotionally processing things surrounding the abuse that just never seemed to go away.

And more importantly, without realizing it, I was dealing with postpartum depression.

At the time, I did not know what that was. I only knew I was struggling to bond with my baby. My oldest was in a Christian daycare during the day, and I would be home with my baby all day and make sure she had everything she needed, but there was minimal cuddling and affection from me to her.

In the evenings, I would either pick up my oldest or have my husband pick her up on his way home, and when my husband got home from work, I would almost immediately find a reason to leave the house. Many times, it was just to go for a drive or walk around Walmart.

Why couldn't I connect with my daughter? Why did I feel numb? I did not know what it was, and I was blaming myself.

Again, more roots of *you are not good enough, capable enough, you are not enough.*

Because my upbringing was more about pushing through and not talking about the real issues, I did not talk about the way I was feeling or the things I noticed about myself. I did not even talk to my husband about them. It is hard for someone to help you when they do not know the problem, or worse, when you tell them there is no problem.

But I was tough, so I would get through this the same way I always had, because I learned early on that I could not truly depend on people. So even when people wanted to help me, my default was, I have to figure this out on my own.

A few months passed, and it was time to make the move to Europe. We said goodbye to our church family and those we had grown close to, took a trip to Mississippi to see my mom, siblings, and two nieces, and then once back in Georgia, we boarded the plane in September of 2011 for what would be home for the next almost four years.

I was not sure what to expect, but like always, I would make it work. Trauma had already taught me how to survive.

What other choice did I have?

New country, new people, same fears, same trauma.

Part 6

Becoming Someone New

CHAPTER 15

A Glimmer of Hope

Even though I didn't know the culture, I knew how to adapt. I had learned early to blend in, fade into the background, and not cause too much commotion in order to keep the peace.

My husband was off to work during the day while I was home with the girls, and I knew nobody there.

His parents worked and were two hours away, so we saw them about once a month. Thankfully, we found out about a local gospel church service on the military base and started going within months of moving there. It was great to have a place to worship, fellowship, and meet new people.

But I did not feel like I belonged.

Many people had been there for a while and already had their friend groups, but then someone encouraged us to attend a marriage covenant night. Though I would have rather found a way to excuse myself, I am glad we went because that night changed the trajectory of my healing journey.

The couple who normally led the marriage covenant group had guest speakers that night, Herb and April, a husband and wife who were American government contractors living in the area. I was so encouraged by their words that I went up to the wife afterward. I did not know her, but I could tell something was different about her.

When we started talking, I discovered that though not exactly the same, she had experienced childhood trauma similar to

mine. And here she was healed, set free, thriving in her marriage, and helping others heal, too.

I wanted to know how to get to that point. I wanted to be free of the nightmares, flashbacks, and fear.

She encouraged me, and we stayed in touch. As it turned out, she attended the same gospel service we had started going to.

Time went on, and I got back into my routine of home life and isolation. It did not help that Germany had a long winter, and if you are not used to that, it can be a bit depressing. So there I was, secretly battling postpartum depression, raising two little ones, at home all day with no adults to talk to, and the woman who understood me lived about an hour away, so seeing her regularly was not an option.

We had one car, and if my husband wasn't using it for work, it often sat in the driveway because I was not yet ready to drive on the German roads.

But I did find motivation for a little while. The on-base gym was doing a Biggest Loser competition, and it motivated me to get back into shape. I think I ended up in the top ten and lost around twenty pounds, which was encouraging for me.

By the time winter was over and spring had come and gone, I decided I no longer wanted to be in the house all the time. Working would be helpful for me. I needed to be around other adults, and since I was still struggling to connect with my second daughter, it would be good for her to be around other children and caring adults.

I started working at the daycare on base, and it was great. Because I already had a background in education, I was able to advance quickly and move into teaching preschool children. My oldest was in preschool by then, and my little one was in the toddler room. Both had caring teachers and caregivers the entire time they were there.

And for me, it gave me something to do and, most importantly, other adults to talk to.

It took me out of isolation and out of my own head, at least for a little while.

I worked my way up and received another promotion within six months of being there. It was great. I was doing well on the job, my kids were thriving, and I even decided to go back to school to work on my master's degree in English.

But I still was not happy or joyful.

When I was with my family, I was there physically, but mentally I was trying to hold it together.

Then I heard about a women's conference Mrs. April and the gospel service were hosting. It would be a full weekend of healing, fellowship, and worship.

I needed to be there, but I had trust issues, and I did not trust people with my children. My husband also had to work, and at the time, I did not know that I could afford the conference.

Mrs. April reached out to me.

"You're coming to the conference, right?"

"I want to, but I don't know."

"Then it's settled. You'll be here, and everything will be fine. Erica, you need to be here."

So I went, and for one of the first times in my life, it was an opportunity to experience the presence of God and see if there was a possibility of me being healed.

CHAPTER 16

A Father God Sent

The conference was great, and the word was powerful, but there was still a barrier between God and me.

Why couldn't I connect with Him the way I knew I was supposed to? What was wrong with me? Why wasn't I as moved spiritually as some of the other women?

Again, the negative self-talk.

While Mrs. April and the team hosted the conference, her husband and some of the other men in the community served the women and made sure things went smoothly.

After one of the nights, Mrs. April's husband, Mr. Herb, was sitting at the table along with about twelve of the women attending the conference. I was one of those women. While we were eating pizza and fellowshipping, he said, "God has shown me, you are my spiritual daughters."

It sounded nice, yet a little strange, because for obvious reasons, I didn't trust men, yet I smiled along with the others and tried to take in the moment before retreating to my room for the night.

I did not realize how deeply those words would take root in me.

Something shifted inside of me that night.

Someone wanted to be my father with no ill intent, expecting nothing in return.

That idea alone felt foreign to me.

The next morning was the last day of the conference, and I woke up with an expectancy that this spiritual father might truly become a father figure in my life.

After we were dismissed, I went and found both Mr. Herb and Mrs. April and said, "I don't know if you really meant what you said last night, but I received it as fact."

They seemed a little tickled by my response, and I remember thinking, *I am so serious.*

We exchanged numbers, he said okay, and we parted for the evening.

When I got back home, I told Josh what had happened and asked him how he felt about me developing this unorthodox father-daughter relationship with Mr. Herb.

He said, "If this is going to help you and you are okay with it, I am fine with it."

I was nervous and excited.

It started out a little awkward because I had never experienced a healthy father-daughter relationship before.

I did not know what normal looked like.

I did not know how often we were supposed to talk, what boundaries existed, or what was expected.

But over time, what once felt unfamiliar became natural.

I shared my background with Mr. Herb and explained that I truly did not know what a healthy father-daughter relationship looked like. He and Mrs. April already had five adult children and a host of spiritual children, so I figured this would be easier for him than for me.

Mrs. April was also on board with all of it, and I was thankful to have her support and encouragement.

I would see his car parked on base and leave him a note. We would talk on the phone about our backstories. He and Mrs. April would counsel Josh and me and even invite us to their home in the local countryside. I even met four of their adult children when they came to visit Herb and April in Germany

It really felt like family.

As time went on, we became so close that they wanted to do a legal adult adoption. The only reason I did not say yes at the time was that it would have meant my mom would have to give up her rights. My mom and I still had, and still have, a great relationship, so I said we did not need adoption paperwork to be family.

My children were so small at the time that they do not remember a time when Granddad and Nana April did not exist.

We became a family, and suddenly a new level of hope was unlocked. Without me even realizing it, God was healing a father wound by allowing me to experience genuine fatherly love with no strings attached and no abuse connected to it.

It was beautiful.

CHAPTER 17

Unlearning What I Was Taught

For the next two years, I had my Daddy Herb and his wife, Mama April, in close proximity, and then in 2013, it was time for them to move back to the States.

I was so distraught.

Lord, You just gave me them. Why are they moving so soon?

I was afraid things would change, that this would not last, that it would not be real.

But what happened next surprised me.

We continued to stay in touch. Unlike my birth father, my Daddy Herb kept his word, and Mama April continued to mentor and counsel me through the early stages of healing when going to a therapist was not even a thought in my mind.

Within months of them leaving, I found out I was pregnant with my third daughter.

I was shocked and afraid.

After the scare of hemorrhaging with my second daughter, Josh and I were concerned. Also, being pregnant would mean I would need to quit my job and be home with my children, and I really loved my job. I knew it was the direction God was leading me toward.

I tried to figure out how to make it work, but by then I had a four-year-old, a two-year-old, and was pregnant with baby girl number three.

I was still struggling and was not sure how God thought I would be able to manage it all.

But I continued to trust Him.

It seemed that having a positive father-daughter relationship with Daddy Herb was helping me have a better view of my heavenly Father, God.

During the pregnancy, we met with specialists in labor and delivery at the German hospital to express my concerns. They assigned me some of the best doctors and midwives and monitored me closely throughout the entire pregnancy.

I do not know when it happened, but I began to notice this pregnancy was different. I was not healed and still had nightmares, flashbacks, and trauma, but I was happier this time around compared to previous pregnancies.

Maybe it was because I had been taking steps toward healing and could see bits and moments of progress.

I was also in some of the best physical health I had been in over the past few years. It was wonderful. I had also made connections with people from work and the gospel service who genuinely cared. I may not have had it all together or all figured out, but I had community, and that was necessary during that season of my life.

Then 2014 came, and so did our third and final daughter.

We were overjoyed and thankful there were no complications. Our youngest came in as the heaviest of our three at eight pounds, fifteen ounces, and though my mom could not be there, I was thankful that my husband's mom was able to step in and take care of my big girls while Josh supported me through labor, delivery, and the early days of recovery.

Life with three became the norm, and though I was exhausted many days, I felt better than before in some ways, but still struggled mentally at times.

Thoughts and fears became unwanted friends who showed up unannounced and stayed far too long.

But now, instead of holding it all in, I was confiding in someone close by who I knew would pray for me and help me work toward healing.

It helped, and I was beginning to see more progress. Then a visit to Mississippi that same year created another layer of healing.

In the summer of 2014, I took my three girls and flew from Germany to Georgia, then drove to Mississippi. My husband was away for training for a month, and I was going to spend time with family.

I was excited to see my mom, little brother, big sister, and my nieces, but I was also nervous.

What if I saw my father? I did not want him to see my girls, but would I be strong enough to tell him no if he tried to ignore my words?

I had not told him I was coming, so that should not have been an issue.

But then one day, while out, I stopped at the post office, the same post office where my father had told me I could not go free ten years before.

My father saw me and stopped over.

He asked if I had my children with me.

I was nervous.

Though I knew I would protect them at all costs, I was still afraid of my father.

Thankfully, my little brother, Jerome, also came by and saw him there. Without me telling him anything, he stepped in and basically let my father know he needed to back up.

And he did.

My little brother protected my girls and me, and God used that moment to redeem the pain of a place once marked with trauma.

And God was not done redeeming time, relationships, and situations.

Then I saw my nephew, the one I had neglected to keep in contact with when I left. He was now a teenager and following in his auntie's footsteps. He was a runner and was doing well in sports.

When I stopped by his house, he shared how I had been the person he admired and looked up to. Not in front of him at that moment, but later, I broke down in tears, overwhelmed that in all those years, he had not chosen to hate me for leaving him with no explanation.

We spent time together, and slowly, over time, that bond began to rebuild.

Now, there were some relationships that were not ready for reconciliation.

Later, while out in town, I saw one of my sisters on my father's side in Walmart. She was one I had confided in years earlier when I said I wanted to press charges. I had not talked to her since that day.

But on this day, my little brother was with me when I saw her, and he was like, "Let's say hello."

He initially wanted to introduce her to my children as their aunt, and I was like, she has not earned the honor of that title.

Yeah, I was not ready.

We were cordial, and just as quickly as we said hello, the conversation was done.

God was also restoring relationships with my big sister and little brother. Not that they were awful, but being isolated from them when young meant we had missed out on sibling bonding. We took a trip to a waterpark, stayed overnight, and brought all the kids. It was the first time in our adulthood that we had been able to do something like that, and we had a great time.

I went back to Germany a little more healed.

But like always, there was something else coming that I would have to make a choice to confront, because ignoring it would no longer be an option.

CHAPTER 18

Survival Mode

In 2015, my family and I received orders to move back to the United States. It would be a new state, somewhere I had never desired to live, and a city I had never even heard of. But by now, Josh and I had learned that if God was sending us somewhere, we would go. After all, He had given me an earthly dad while we were in Germany. What would He do here?

By that point, I had learned that sometimes God moves you physically before He moves you emotionally. I left Germany grateful for what God had done there, but I still carried wounds that had not fully healed.

Maryland, where we lived, and Texas, where Daddy Herb lived, were several hours apart, but that did not stop anything. Because he traveled often for work and his wife traveled with him, they would stop by to visit us in Maryland whenever they were in the area.

After moving to Maryland, I wanted to jump right into the workforce. I had been a stay-at-home mom for over two years, and to be honest, I was over that life. I wanted to talk with real adults, enjoy my food without having to share it, and take bathroom breaks without interruptions.

I applied and applied and applied.

No one wanted to hire me.

Maybe.

Or maybe God was simply trying to help me realize that it was not the right time for me to rejoin the workforce. There were still lessons He wanted to teach me, show me, and reveal to me—but He could not do that if I was overly distracted with a full-time job.

During this waiting period, I was depressed, but I do not think I fully realized it at the time.

I would get up to take my oldest to school and then return home. My two youngest would go to daycare for a few hours twice a week, and when they did, I would sleep. I would feed them lunch when they returned home, and then we would all sleep again.

Later, I would pick up my oldest from school and allow the girls to play in the house or watch TV while I lay on the couch or surf the web. I would prepare dinner, but that was about it.

By the time Josh got home, the house was not clean, the laundry was not done, the dishes were piled high, and toys were not put away.

Looking back, I am shocked at how things were.

At the time, I did not recognize it as depression. I simply thought I was tired, overwhelmed, and failing at things other mothers seemed to manage just fine.

After a while, I was not only struggling to maintain our house and take care of our girls, but I was also struggling mentally to hold it all together. It was rough, but it was also the point when we realized something had to change—and quickly.

You see, being home with three small children all day—watching cartoons, changing diapers, wiping bottoms, kissing boo-boos, fixing meals, and having constant kiddie conversations—was my life.

I had no time for myself, very little sleep, and no real outlet.

I was a prisoner of my own home, and I did not even realize it.

I loved my children deeply, but loving them did not mean I knew how to take care of myself.

If someone was sick, I did not sleep. There were no "me days." I did not even know what that was back then. I simply existed to be there for everyone else. Plus, I was still in school getting a graduate degree in English.

The problem with that mindset was that there was nobody there for me.

Everything felt stressful and unenjoyable. I did not enjoy hearing their crying, excessive laughter, fighting, or anything that felt unnecessary to me in that moment. And I felt terrible for feeling that way.

But by then, I had become very skilled at telling myself everything I was doing wrong.

I learned to cope.

I existed, but I was rarely ever present.

I did not enjoy playing with my children or spending time with my husband. Mentally, I was somewhere else entirely.

And then I began to ask myself hard questions.

What about the other relationships in my life?
Was I still angry with my biological father?
My sisters, who I felt had abandoned me?
Or was I angry with myself for not knowing how to help myself?

Then in 2016, things began to change internally in ways that could not be ignored.

I had just finished my master's degree. I had started a new job in a supervisory position at a childcare center on base, and I was about to begin my career as a college instructor. All three of my girls were thriving. We had finally settled into a church in the Maryland area, and I had even reconnected with a friend from Georgia who was also stationed in Maryland at the time.

From the outside, everything looked good.

But internally, I was still running.

I was working nearly three jobs simultaneously, back in school for yet another degree, and still feeling like a failure as a mom and a wife.

I was trying to show up for everyone, but in reality, I was showing up for no one—not even myself.

I was barely getting any sleep, and I began to regret the life I had built.

God started allowing me to see—even though I did not fully understand yet—that major healing would need to take place in my life.

2016 was the year I hit a level of rock bottom mentally, where daily mental battles became an unfortunate norm. I knew I needed help. But I also knew that growing up where I was from, Black people did not do therapy, at least not the ones I knew.

So what was I supposed to do?

For the first time in my life, I had to admit that prayer alone was not going to erase the wounds I had been carrying since childhood.

Around that time, I began reading a book called *Heart Made Whole* by Christa Black Gifford. It addressed trauma, emotional wounds, and the necessity of healing.

The questions in that book forced me to confront parts of my past I had avoided for years.

I was angry.

I was an adult, but in many ways, I still felt like a child. For much of my life, someone else had always spoken for me, thought for me, and decided for me.

Now I was an adult—wife, mother, and college instructor—who still felt like a child internally.

I looked at my children and realized I had not been much older than them when the abuse started.

That realization brought another wave of anger.

But God helped me process it the best way I could at the time.

That book opened another layer of healing for me. It forced me to stop pretending I was fine and begin asking questions I had spent years avoiding.

There were several times when I wanted to throw the book across the room because the memories it stirred up were so gut-wrenching. I felt an overwhelming amount of emotions that I did not yet have language for.

But with God's help, I kept going.

My husband gave me the space to process without judgment.

When I finished the book, I knew there was still more work to do.

But for the first time in my life, I was willing.

CHAPTER 19

When Healing Began

Though I was not fully healed and very aware of that, I felt like God wanted to use me to help others. I began to dream again and felt hope on a level I don't think I had ever felt before. It felt good to hope, to feel positive, to feel like I could make a difference.

I reached out to one of the pastors at our church and shared my thoughts about this book I had recently read, and asked what steps I should take next. She told me to sign up to be a group leader. It was new and a little intimidating, but it turned out to be one of the best decisions I could have made at the time.

It gave me purpose and a place to share a small piece of my testimony—a safe space. There I was, leading a women's group and helping other people heal.

It felt good to see that God was beginning to give me beauty for ashes in a way that I could actually see and understand in the moment. That one act of faith—to reach out and pursue what I felt God placing on my heart—would lead to more healing and more opportunities for God to do His mighty work in my life and in the lives of others.

By this time, I also had a mentor who was another pastor on staff at my church. I had shared some of my story with her, and it was clear that I was not fully healed. I thank God for giving her the discernment and wisdom to say what she said next with the gentleness and compassion that made it easy to receive.

"Have you ever considered seeing a psychologist? I think it would be good for you."

She then recommended that I watch the movie *The Shack*.

The movie had been out for a while, and I found a theatre that was still playing it. I went to watch the movie by myself, and in a theatre where maybe four other people were also there, God met me. I was not prepared for the level of emotion I would feel or the quiet sense of "Okay, God" that settled in my spirit by the end of it.

Then, as recommended, I reached out to the psychologist.

During the initial consultation, she asked me about my backstory and what had brought me to seek support. I told her about my childhood, what I had gone through, and where I currently was in life.

She seemed surprised, and her response made that clear.

"How are you still making it? How are you still sane?"

My answer was simple.

By the grace of God.

Even though my relationship with Him still felt a little rocky at times, I knew He was the reason I had made it through everything I had endured and carried for so many years.

She agreed to take me on as a client, and I began seeing her regularly for therapy.

It was challenging at first.

Because I had spent most of my life people-pleasing and trying to say and do everything "right," I was not sure how to approach therapy. I assumed there was a right way to talk, a right way to answer questions, a right way to heal.

She wanted none of that.

She would often tell me, "Leave your expectations at the door."

In other words, she wanted me to walk into the room open to whatever God wanted to do during that session rather than trying to control it.

I walked into therapy carrying years of guilt and shame, as if what had happened to me had somehow been my fault.

I felt responsible for not knowing it was wrong.
For not realizing I had been manipulated and brainwashed.
For believing the lies my father told me.
For not knowing how to say no.
For not knowing I had a choice.
For allowing my voice to be silenced for so long.

As you can see, I came into therapy with every dagger pointed directly at myself.

She helped me begin to release all of it.

And then she began helping me understand something I had never truly believed before.

What happened to me was not my fault.

The shame I carried did not belong to me.

Healing was possible.

Slowly, I began to realize that I could make decisions for myself.

I began to understand that I had been powerless against my father and the other men who took advantage of me as a child. I had been taught incorrect ideas about my body and what it was meant for, and those lies had deeply impacted how I saw myself.

As a child, I had not known that I could say no. I had not known that refusing someone was even an option.

There is a difference between choosing not to say no and being unable to say no because you were never taught that you could.

Through therapy, I also began to realize that I did not truly love myself. The words others had spoken over me, the way I had been treated, and the way I believed God must have felt about me had convinced me that I was not worthy of love or true affection.

And when people did try to show genuine affection, I often viewed it with suspicion.

My immediate thought was, *What do you want from me?* Or, *What is your ulterior motive?*

Time went on, and I continued doing the work of healing.

Some sessions were harder than others.

Like the time she challenged me about why I visited Mississippi so often. I believed it was simply what I was supposed to do. But she asked me to consider how damaging it might be to constantly revisit the place where my deepest wounds were formed when those wounds had not yet healed.

Though I did not want to accept it at first, I eventually realized that I had been returning to Mississippi out of an unspoken sense of obligation.

The two places I once called home held trauma and memories of unspeakable moments.

Every time I visited, I felt anxious. At the time, I did not understand that the anxiety was my body signaling that it did not feel safe.

Moments like that made me grateful that I had started therapy—but they also made me nervous about what else might surface as I continued the journey.

There were days when I wondered if I would go back.

Therapy was forcing me to become uncomfortable. It required honesty about areas of my life I had kept tucked away, hidden but still loud, quietly influencing my life for more than a decade.

The discomfort of healing was painful.

But so was staying traumatized.

The difference was that staying traumatized was familiar. Healing was not.

No one had told me how painful healing could be.

But by that point, I had already begun opening wounds that had been buried for years, and I could not simply walk away and leave them exposed.

I had to continue the work.

And I was beginning to understand something important.

If God reveals an area of your life that needs healing, it is often because He is ready to walk with you through it.

Part 7

Living What I Fought For

CHAPTER 20

Learning to Play

Healing was hard work.

I had become so numb over the years—isolated and silent—that when it was time to begin changing, even the simplest things felt unfamiliar.

I remember one day my girls wanted to play. I didn't have the energy or motivation, and I told them honestly,
"Mommy doesn't know how to play, girls. My childhood was different."

They didn't get upset.

Quite the opposite.

"It's okay, Mommy," they said. "We can teach you."

Three girls between the ages of two and seven were going to teach me how to play.

At first, I watched them more than I played. But slowly, it changed. Tea parties, dolls, little games on the floor. Regular trips to the park. Things I had never really experienced growing up were now happening on a normal basis, and it was beautiful to witness.

I used to wonder why God would give me daughters when I wasn't even sure I would know how to help them. Moments like that reminded me that He was healing me through them, too.

Being their mother was healing areas in me that had been waiting for years to exhale and relax.

During that time, I also adjusted the frequency of my visits back home while I continued doing the work of healing. I knew I would still return for visits, but on my schedule, and now I needed a safety plan.

If I didn't feel safe, where was the closest hotel?

What would I say if someone asked why I didn't want to stay at home instead?

How would I respond to comments like, "We hardly see you anymore?"

I was learning to protect my peace.

At the same time, I was developing meaningful relationships at church, and I had slowed down in the work department, being mindful not to take on too much. I had also finished school, again, and was planning to take an extended break this time.

Because I was no longer running from my issues but actually confronting them, I didn't feel the need to overdo things the way I once had.

Though things weren't perfect, they were definitely getting better.

God was even going to answer what had felt like a silent prayer in my life.

"Lord, bring me true friends."

You see, I would often hear people say things like:

"This has been my best friend since second grade."
"We've known each other for over twenty years."
"We've been best friends since high school."

I didn't feel like I had that.

Not fully.

I didn't realize that God intended to heal that area of my life, too.

Around that time, I had recently joined a gym and was having a great time. It was an all-women's gym, and the ladies there were so encouraging and kind. I knew one person who went there, but we didn't usually go together.

One day, while out with my family picking up something to eat from a local bakery, I felt the Lord prompt me to speak to a woman who was inside the bakery, sitting off to the side of the room.

Mind you, I didn't know this woman, and I was not quick to walk up and start conversations with strangers. But the prompting of the Lord was strong.

I grabbed our order and took it out to the car. I told my husband I needed to go back inside because I felt God leading me to speak to someone.

Because he knew me, he didn't question it.

A simple "okay," and I walked back in.

I approached the woman and said,
"Hi, I'm Erica. I see you're reading the book I'm currently reading, too."

She smiled.

"I'm Shawnte. Nice to meet you."

We talked for a few minutes and realized she had just joined the same gym I attended. We decided we would take a class together sometime.

I went back to the car feeling grateful that I had spoken to her. I didn't know what would come of it, but at least I had been obedient.

To my surprise, she showed up for the class.

We exchanged contact information and started talking more. It turned out she lived less than five minutes from me, had three boys in the same age range as my three girls, and she was cheerful all the time.

That last part took some getting used to.

I wasn't used to people being that cheerful, that joyful about life.

But we continued to spend time together, eventually even getting our husbands and kids together.

Then she told me about another friend she had, Dorina.

Dorina seemed quiet and serious at first. She appeared to be the opposite of Shawnte, or so I thought. But we actually had quite a bit in common.

She also had three children—two boys and a girl—and they were close in age to my girls.

At first, I mostly saw Dorina when Shawnte was around, but over time, Dorina and I began warming up to each other. I realized that her quiet strength was not a negative.

And she really wasn't that quiet after all.

Once we discovered that we all loved the Lord, our friendship deepened even more.

We could openly talk about Jesus, share our concerns, ask each other for prayer, and know it was genuine and mutual.

We continued cultivating our friendship, talking often.

Like every day, often.

I couldn't believe it.

It almost felt too good to be true.

I had real friends—true friends—as an adult. Women who knew about my past and still wanted to be part of my life.

"Okay, God," I remember thinking. "Thank You."

After a while, we even formed our own date-night babysitting rotation. Each of us would take turns watching the other person's children so the couples could go out on a date.

It was wonderful to have women I trusted watching my children so I could go out with my husband without worrying about their safety.

Then came something I had only ever seen in movies.

A girls' trip.

We decided to go to the Poconos for a weekend. Our kids and their fathers would survive a few days without us, right?

Right.

We piled into my van and drove the three and a half hours to the mountains.

And in typical fashion, we talked the entire way.

It was fantastic.

When we arrived at the resort, we settled in and started learning more about each other's habits—sleeping preferences, food routines, and all the little things that make people unique.

It was enlightening and fun.

We went to a Hibachi restaurant where the chef was more comedian than cook, which helped because the food was not our favorite that night. That may have been because we had a favorite Hibachi restaurant back in Maryland that we frequented, and comparison was not our friend that evening.

We went to the movies and quickly realized we all had different definitions of what was actually funny.

We found a donut shop and indulged a little.

We didn't sleep much, but we laughed a lot and made memories that weekend.

We found a waterfall and took pictures with it as our backdrop. We walked a trail and sat together overlooking the river and mountains.

We prayed.

We laughed.

And somewhere in the middle of that trip, God healed another small piece of my heart.

He reminded me that He could be trusted.

And slowly, I was learning that I could trust Him.

CHAPTER 21

When God Gave Me the Vision

Healing is a journey, and I was beginning to realize it was not one with a quick fix. Almost every healing victory felt earned through tears, overcoming fears, and fighting against the lies of the enemy and the doubts that often filled my mind. It wasn't perfect, but the journey was mine.

Through it all, God continued to show me that He wanted me to do something more with my story. The idea of a nonprofit began forming in my mind—an organization that would help adult survivors of childhood sexual abuse feel seen, heal, and overcome the pain of their past in the safety of others who had already walked a similar road of healing.

I was excited, but I was also scared. This would be a huge undertaking. I had so many thoughts about how it could work and the kind of impact it could make, but I also wrestled with doubt. Questions flooded my mind. Who would support this? Who would help me? Am I healed enough for this?

Still, the excitement remained, and I decided to share the idea with a mentor and ask for their thoughts. I just knew they would be excited too. Instead, I left that conversation feeling like a balloon that had been deflated. They said it was a good idea, but they could not support it at the time.

Immediately, comparison crept in and began having a field day in my mind. They supported other people's projects. Why not mine?

Maybe I'm not ready.

For a moment, I believed the lies.

But God wasn't finished.

Soon after, I discovered an organization that was helping some of the same women I had a heart to serve. I found the contact information for the founder and reached out to her. To my surprise, she was willing to speak with me about the process and encouraged me in the journey toward helping other women. She even offered me the opportunity to partner with her organization instead of starting my own.

I was grateful for her kindness and generosity, but deep down I knew that God had placed something different in my heart. Because I still felt unsure of what to do next—and unsure of who would support it—I slowed down my movement toward the vision. The idea remained alive, but I delayed pursuing it fully for a few more years.

That experience taught me something important. Not everyone will see the vision the way God gave it to you, and because of that, they may not recognize the opportunity for what it truly is. That does not mean you give up. Sometimes it simply means you must be more selective about who gets to walk with you on the journey God has called you to.

I continued doing the healing work while quietly building in the background, little by little, toward the nonprofit.

Around that same time, I had also started my own editing company, Joyful Editing Services, and it was doing well. I learned early on that trauma has a way of showing up—even in business—if it has not been addressed. One of the lessons I had to learn was that it was okay to say no to potential clients because not every client is a good client. I had a couple of learning moments early on, but thankfully, I caught the lesson quickly.

Business was going well, work was manageable, and life was beginning to feel stable in ways it had not before. Daddy Herb and Mama April continued to visit often enough, and even Josh's parents had moved back stateside, so we were able to see them occasionally as well. My mom was also visiting regularly, and I would travel to Mississippi when it felt right. I was no longer going out of a false sense of obligation.

During this season, my therapist began transitioning her practice and would no longer be seeing clients in the area where I lived. I was sad to see that chapter end, but I was also grateful for the work we had done together and the healing that had begun during that time. I knew I could not stop now.

I began researching and eventually found another therapist who seemed like a possible fit. Still, I was hesitant. Something felt slightly off. I knew she was not my previous therapist, and I knew it was unfair to expect them to be exactly the same, but I still was not fully convinced.

If you know anything about therapy, you know that if you are not comfortable with your therapist, growth becomes much harder. Vulnerability requires trust. Even so, I decided to give it a try.

The attempt was short-lived.

Partly because of the global pandemic and another military move.

In 2020, the world shut down, but the military did not. They still needed us to move for a special assignment in Texas.

I said, "See you later" to Shawnte, Dorina, and their families, packed up our home once again, and we began the transition from Maryland to Texas.

By that point, Daddy Herb and Mama April had already moved on to Nevada, so once again, we were heading to a new place where we did not know anyone.

But deep down, I still felt that there was more God wanted to do.

And I was finally beginning to trust more in His plan for my journey.

CHAPTER 22

The Letter

I was finally able to live out what my first therapist, Dr. N, meant when she said to visit without a sense of obligation.

Josh had to stay behind in Maryland to finish some training, so it was just going to be the girls and me for that portion of the trip. Josh's mom was amazing and flew into Maryland to ride down to Georgia with me so I wouldn't have to make that long drive alone with the girls.

As we made the drive from Maryland to Texas, we stopped at a few places along the way. Being that we had been living in Maryland at the onset of COVID, we were used to being locked in—minimal visitation with friends and very little contact with anyone who did not live inside our home. By June of 2020, when we were headed to our next duty station, I could feel the weight of that isolation.

Once we arrived in Georgia, everything felt peaceful.

We stayed there for about a week and spent time with my mother and father-in-law.

Remember, I am from Mississippi, and southern cooking is just good. One of the blessings in my life is that my father-in-law is also from Mississippi, so he knew exactly how to make the kind of comfort food that felt like home—only he made it in healthier ways. I was grateful.

My mother-in-law entertained her granddaughters and allowed me to rest. It was wonderful. Being around people I trusted with my children made resting possible.

Since we were so close to Mississippi, I knew we had to go there too. More importantly, I wanted to go. I was missing my family.

I spent time at my mom's house, but most of my time was actually spent at my sister's home with my nieces and my little nephew, the newest addition to our family.

We made so many memories. Took so many pictures.

Even though we could not go out and do all the things we normally might have because of COVID restrictions, we made the most of the time we had. We had dance parties and laughed a lot. We had in-house sleepovers and long conversations that lasted late into the night.

I needed that.

When it was time to hit the road again and continue the drive to Texas, I was ready—but not in a "get me out of here" kind of way. It was the kind of readiness that comes after your heart has been filled.

By then, Josh had driven in and met us in Mississippi so we could finish the trip together. On our way west, we stopped in Little Rock, Arkansas, to rest before completing the final leg of the journey.

To our surprise, Tracey stopped by to see us. It had been quite some time since we had seen each other in person, but it felt like hardly any time had passed at all. My girls were excited to see their godmother, and even though we kept the visit short because of COVID precautions, it was meaningful and special.

The next day, we finished the drive and arrived in Texas.

We settled in quickly, but before long, we were packing our bags again. This time, we were headed to Nevada to see Daddy Herb and Mama April.

When we arrived, they welcomed us with open arms. It had been several months since we had seen each other, and that was far too long. We spent quality time together, and my girls were thrilled to see their grandparents. I was just as happy to see my dad and spend time with Mama April.

God was giving me exactly what I needed.

Strong bonds.

Within the span of about a month, my girls had seen all of their grandparents, and I had been surrounded by love in every direction.

After our travels, we returned to Texas and began settling into life there. Because COVID was still very prevalent, we made the decision to homeschool all three girls that year.

I was a teacher, so I figured, how hard could it be?

Honestly, it wasn't too complicated. The hardest part was probably trying to keep them entertained since field trips and outings were not as easy during that season.

But something beautiful happened that year.

Family became even more important.

It seemed to rise higher on the priority list for all of us.

That Thanksgiving, my mom, my sister, and her family, and one of my cousins all came to visit. The time together was meaningful and joyful. I was able to show up as myself—no pretending, no hiding—just existing with family in a healthy way.

The following year, in 2021, homeschooling allowed me the flexibility to travel back to Mississippi for an important event. My oldest niece was preparing for her junior prom, and I wanted to be there.

My girls and I made the eight-hour drive. Josh stayed behind in Texas since he still had to report to work regularly.

I loved helping my niece shop for her dress and watching her prepare for prom. It was a beautiful moment to witness.

But I also knew this trip was not just about family fun.

There was something else I needed to do.

Something the Lord had been preparing my heart for.

This part of the trip would be different.

I was nervous. A little anxious. But deep down, I knew I would be okay.

I needed to confront my father.

Not in anger. Not in hostility.

But for years on this healing journey, there were still things from that part of my past that caused me to question whether I had truly forgiven.

Being honest, I was still afraid of him.

Even though I had not seen him in years.

Even though I had not spoken to him in about a year.

For a long time after the abuse ended, I still felt that being a "good Christian daughter" meant calling him on his birthday each year and telling him happy birthday.

But this time felt different.

This time, I felt the need to return to the place where it all began.

Silenced No More

His house.

I didn't know what the conversation would look like. I didn't even know if he would listen if I tried to say everything that had been sitting in my heart for so many years.

So I wrote a letter and made a copy of it.

I wrote everything down.

Sixteen pages later, I was finished. Every memory, every question, every word I had carried for years was finally on paper.

I wasn't angry.

I was choosing to release whatever residue, bitterness, or unforgiveness might still have remained.

The day finally came.

I didn't call ahead.

Truthfully, I was afraid.

I don't think I had been back to that house since I left in 2008.

Before leaving to deliver the letter, I told my mom what I was going to do. She seemed disturbed and concerned, but I told her I needed to do this.

I got in my car and began driving.

Pray.

Drive.

Repeat.

Before I arrived, I called one of my father's sons—my oldest brother—to let him know what I was about to do. We had reconnected more in the past year, and I knew he lived nearby in case something went wrong.

He stayed on the phone with me until I arrived at the driveway.

I pulled up and sat there for a moment.

I had no intention of going into the house.

I didn't need to.

Eventually, my father came out and walked up the hill toward where I had parked.

What I saw was not the same man I had feared for so many years.

Instead, I saw a frail version of him, just shy of 80 years old.

He looked surprised to see me.

And strangely, the overwhelming fear I had felt just minutes earlier was gone.

We spoke briefly.

Nothing dramatic.

Nothing loud.

Just words.

Around that time, my mom called and said, "You need to come back now. You have to get on the road soon to head back to Texas."

Deep down, I knew what she really meant.

She was worried.

Different words, same message.

My brother called to check on me, and I assured him that I was okay.

Before I backed out of the driveway, I handed him the letter.

Then I drove back to my mom's house.

I don't know if he ever read the letter, but it didn't matter.

The woman who pulled out of that driveway was not the same one who had pulled into it earlier.

I was freer.

More healed.

Though I had forgiven in part over the years, this time it was finished.

And I knew it.

That level of forgiveness demanded healing happen.

It demanded change.

It broke chains I had carried for years and released a level of freedom I did not know was possible from what seemed like such a simple act of obedience.

And deep down I knew: this is what healing looks like.

CHAPTER 23

Walking in Freedom

Forgiveness truly opens the door for wonders to happen.

It has been five years since I delivered that letter to my father, and although everything has not been perfect, it has certainly been better. I returned from that trip focused on walking out my purpose, no longer chained to my past.

Soon after returning, I completed my teacher certification program for the state of Texas and began teaching at a high school with amazing students, whom I was able to impact for a season. I taught ninth graders for a year, and many of them told me I was a great teacher but believed my true calling was to be a counselor. That made me smile because it meant they knew I cared about them as whole people and not just for what they produced in my classroom. It was also a reminder that God will use others to confirm a calling in you.

Later, I began teaching high school seniors, and they helped heal layers of little Erica that I did not even realize were still hurting. Helping these students make decisions about their futures and watching them step into life without fear was freeing for me. They were doing things I had never been able to do at their age, and they invited me along for their journeys. They were pretty special.

While teaching, I continued building the nonprofit in the background. In 2022, Overcoming 2 Become was officially established to provide a safe space for adult survivors of childhood sexual abuse to heal and grow in community with safe people.

The name was important. It serves as a reminder that we are all overcoming on the journey to become who we were always meant to be.

Today, we continue looking for ways to support survivors and their families through courses, community, and resources as we expand our reach.

During this time, Joyful Editing Services, my editing business, also continued to grow. What began as a small service eventually expanded into a publishing company, Pen to Paper Publishing, where I also serve as an author coach and consultant.

Eventually, I left the high school classroom and transitioned into full-time collegiate teaching, something I have been happily doing for over three years now.

As a mom and a wife, I still do not always get everything right, but I am much more present than I used to be. Tea parties and park playdates have now transitioned into spa days and Hallmark movies at home with popcorn.

I am thankful that I get to watch my husband and our three girls have healthy father-daughter relationships.

I have also shared my story with thousands of people through social media, speaking engagements, small groups, and other spaces where survivors gather.

There is still healing to be done, but I know I am much further ahead than where I started this journey over ten years ago.

I still attend therapy and have now worked with the same Christian therapist, who specializes in sexual abuse trauma, for the past four years.

Through that work, I have learned a great deal about myself and how my father's misuse of God and religion twisted my understanding of who God truly is. His actions distorted my relationship with God and my perception of what it meant to be a good Christian.

Unlearning those false beliefs so I could learn the truth has been a significant part of my healing journey.

Who knew unlearning could be so complicated?

But I remain persistent and committed to healing for the long haul.

Because I also wanted my children to grow up with a healthy understanding of therapy, each of them had the opportunity to work with a therapist as well. I allowed them to have a say about who their therapist would be because I needed them to feel comfortable with the person they would trust with their stories.

Regarding friendships, even though we now live in different states, Shawnte, Dorina, and I still communicate regularly and have continued our tradition of girls' trips over the past several years.

I have also learned to prioritize self-care in ways I never did before. One of the books that helped deepen my understanding was *The Body Keeps the Score*, a book about trauma by Bessel van der Kolk, which helped me understand how the body works to protect us and also signals to us when something is not right— even when we do not realize that is what it is doing.

When I look at the version of myself today, I see someone vastly different from the woman I was ten years ago… even five years ago.

Healing will do that to you.

And finally, I wrote the book—this book you are reading right now.

For years, God placed it on my heart. I would start writing, and then life would happen, or I would put it off. Other times, more healing still needed to take place. But even through the pauses, I never gave up on this book.

Because this book is evidence that my voice is no longer silenced.

This book is hope for another survivor that healing is possible.

This book is a reminder to me of the many things God has brought me out of.

This book is obedience in action.

This book is for His glory.

For years, my story lived in silence, but today I share it in the hope that someone else finds the courage to begin their own healing journey.

If you are reading this and carrying pain from your own past, I want you to know that healing is possible. It may not happen quickly, and it may not happen in the way you expect, but it is possible. Your story does not end with what was done to you.

There is life, purpose, and freedom waiting on the other side of the healing journey.

For many years, I believed my story was one of shame and silence. Today, I know it is a story of redemption. God did not waste my pain. He met me in it, walked with me through it, and continues to use it to help others find their way toward healing.

And today, I can say with confidence what once felt impossible:

I really am Silenced No More!

Forgiveness Does Not Always Equal Reconciliation

Years have passed since some of the events I shared in this book took place. Over time, through my relationship with Jesus, counseling, and wise counsel from others, I have learned an important truth: love plus forgiveness does not automatically equal reconciliation.

My mom and I are now in a healthy place in our relationship as mother and daughter. We talk often and have regularly scheduled visits.

When it comes to my two remaining siblings who grew up in the home with my mom and me, they are still present in my adulthood. Though they did not know every detail at first, over the years, we have had honest conversations about what I lived through, the healing journey I have been on, and the good God has brought from my story to encourage other survivors. We are older and wiser now, and we can bring our real selves into the sibling space without having to pretend.

As for my father, I am able to pray for him and check on him by phone or through a relative, as the Lord leads. When I say I forgave him, I mean it.

On my father's side, I was also able to reconnect with an older sibling whom I had only briefly known about growing up. It has been a blessing to get to know him and for him to get to know the real me.

As for the others, I have learned not to force relationships.

That does not mean I do not have hope, because I do.

But I also understand that the version of me some people knew years ago was not the real me, and I cannot go back to who I was.

Whatever happens from here, I believe God is able.

He can breathe new life into relationships when all parties are willing.

And He can bring peace even when reconciliation is not possible.

Today, I choose to trust God with the outcome.

I can love.

I can forgive.

And in some stories, that has to be enough.

Acknowledgments

There are many people who have walked beside me on this journey, and I am deeply grateful for each of you.

First and foremost, I thank God. His grace, patience, and faithfulness carried me through seasons I once believed I would never survive. This story is ultimately a testimony of His ability to bring healing, restoration, and purpose out of pain.

To my husband and children, thank you for your love, patience, and encouragement. Your presence in my life has been a constant reminder that healing leads to new beginnings. You have given me countless reasons to keep growing, keep believing, and keep moving forward.

To the friends who became safe places in my life, thank you for showing me what genuine care, trust, and healthy relationships look like. Your encouragement and willingness to walk beside me in both the hard moments and the joyful ones have meant more than words can fully express.

To the counselors, mentors, and trusted voices who helped guide me through the healing process, thank you for the wisdom, compassion, and patience you extended along the way. Your work made it possible for me to see that healing is not only necessary, but possible.

To the survivors who have shared pieces of their own stories with me over the years, thank you for your courage. Your honesty and strength continue to inspire me and remind me why this work matters.

And finally, to the reader holding this book, thank you for being here. Whether you picked up this story out of curiosity, compassion, or because parts of it feel familiar, I pray these pages remind you that silence does not have the final word and that healing is always worth pursuing.

About the Author

Erica Trinette Young is an author, educator, and advocate committed to helping others find healing, purpose, and freedom through faith and truth.

As a survivor of childhood sexual abuse, Erica understands firsthand the long and often complex journey of healing. Through counseling, faith, and the support of safe people, she began the work of reclaiming her voice and rebuilding her life. Today, she shares her story to encourage other survivors to know that healing is possible and that their past does not have to define their future.

Erica is the founder of **Overcoming 2 Become**, a nonprofit organization created to support adult survivors of childhood sexual abuse by providing safe spaces for healing, community, and growth. Through courses, mentorship, and resources, the organization seeks to remind survivors that they are not alone and that freedom is possible.

In addition to her advocacy work, Erica is an educator who has taught both high school and collegiate English courses. She currently serves as a college instructor, where she continues to encourage students to discover their voices and pursue their purpose.

Erica is also the founder of **Pen to Paper Publishing**, where she works as an editor, author coach, and publishing consultant. Through this work, she helps writers bring their stories to life with dignity and grace.

She lives in Texas with her husband and their children. When she is not teaching, writing, or working with authors, Erica

enjoys spending time with her family, reading, and continuing her own journey of growth and healing.

Silenced No More is her testimony that God can bring beauty from even the deepest pain and that no story is too broken to be redeemed.

To learn more about Erica's work, visit:

www.ericatrinette.com

About Pen to Paper Publishing

Pen to Paper Publishing was created to help writers bring their stories to life with clarity, purpose, and impact.

Founded by author, educator, and editor Erica Young, the publishing company supports writers who feel called to share their experiences, messages, and expertise through books that inspire, encourage, and empower others.

Through editing, author coaching, and publishing guidance, Pen to Paper Publishing helps writers move from idea to finished manuscript while maintaining authenticity and integrity in their voice. The goal is not simply to produce books, but to help authors create meaningful work that can change lives.

Many of the stories supported through Pen to Paper Publishing come from individuals who have overcome significant life challenges and want to use their experiences to bring hope and encouragement to others.

At its core, Pen to Paper Publishing believes that stories matter—and that the right story shared at the right time can make a lasting difference.

To learn more about author coaching, editing services, or publishing support, visit:

www.ericatrinette.com

Resources for Survivors

If parts of this story felt familiar to you, please know that you are not alone.

Survivors of abuse often carry their pain in silence for many years. Speaking about it, seeking support, and beginning the healing process can feel overwhelming. But healing is possible, and there are people and organizations who care deeply and are ready to help.

If you are currently experiencing abuse or are struggling with the effects of past trauma, consider reaching out to a trusted counselor, a safe friend or family member, or a professional support organization.

Below are a few resources that provide confidential support and information for survivors.

RAINN (Rape, Abuse & Incest National Network)
RAINN operates the National Sexual Assault Hotline and provides support, information, and resources for survivors of sexual violence.
Hotline: **800-656-HOPE (4673)**
Website: **www.rainn.org**

National Sexual Violence Resource Center (NSVRC)
Provides education, resources, and information for survivors, advocates, and communities working to prevent sexual violence.
Website: **www.nsvrc.org**

SAMHSA National Helpline
A confidential treatment referral and information service for

individuals facing mental health or trauma-related challenges.

Helpline: **1-800-662-HELP (4357)**
Website: **www.samhsa.gov**

If you are outside the United States, many countries have similar organizations that provide support and confidential services for survivors.

You may also consider seeking support through faith-based counseling, trauma-informed therapy, or local survivor support groups.

Healing is not a straight path, and it often requires time, patience, and safe people. But your story does not end with what was done to you.

If you would like to learn more about resources and community support for survivors, you can also visit:

Overcoming 2 Become
A nonprofit organization created to support adult survivors of childhood sexual abuse through healing resources, community, and encouragement.
Website: **www.overcoming2become.org**

Stay Connected

Thank you for reading *The Lost Woman: Silenced No More.*

If this story encouraged you, challenged you, or reminded you that healing is possible, I would love to stay connected with you.

You can learn more about my work, upcoming projects, and resources for healing and growth by visiting my website:

www.ericatrinette.com

There you will find information about:

• Overcoming 2 Become — a nonprofit supporting adult survivors of childhood sexual abuse
• Author coaching and publishing support through Pen to Paper Publishing
• speaking engagements and upcoming books
• additional resources for healing and personal growth

You can also connect with me on social media, where I regularly share encouragement, faith-centered reflections, and conversations about healing and purpose.

If this book resonated with you, one of the most helpful things you can do is leave a review where you purchased the book. Your review helps other readers discover stories that may bring them hope and encouragement.

Thank you for taking this journey with me.

— Erica Young